The Rock House Method

Presents

PIANO

Master Edition

Written & Method By
John McCarthy

Adapted By: Jimmy Rutkowski
Supervising Editor: John McCarthy
Music Transcribing & Engraving: Jimmy Rutkowski
Production Manager: John McCarthy
Technical Consultant: Sal Grillo
Layout, Graphics & Design: Jimmy Rutkowski
Photography: Rodney Dabney & Jimmy Rutkowski
Copy Editor: Cathy McCarthy
Audio Examples: Sal Grillo

Cover Art Direction & Design:
Jimmy Rutkowski

HL250951
Produced by McCarthy Publishing®
© 2018 John McCarthy, All Rights Reserved

Table of Contents

Level 2 Starts at Page 52   Level 3 Starts at Page 99

Key Tab Starts Page 144

Member Number Page 186

Icon Key

These tell you there is additional information and learning utilities available at RockHouseMethod.com to support that lesson.

Backing Track

Backing track icons are placed on lessons where there is an audio demonstration to let you hear what that lesson should sound like or a backing track to play the lesson over. Use these audio tracks to guide you through the lessons. **Use your member number at the back of the book to download the corresponding audio tracks from the *Lesson Support* site.**

Metronome

Metronome icons are placed next to the examples that we recommend you practice using a metronome. You can download a free, adjustable metronome on the *Lesson Support* site.

Quiz

Each level of the curriculum contains multiple quizzes to gauge your progress. When you see a quiz icon go to the Lesson Support site and take the quiz. It will be graded and emailed to you for review.

Worksheet

Worksheets are a great tool to help you thoroughly learn and understand music. These worksheets can be downloaded at the *Lesson Support* site.

Tuner

You can download the free online tuner on the *Lesson Support* site to help tune your instrument.

Digital eBook

When you register this product at the lesson support site you will receive a digital version of this book. This interactive eBook can be used on all devices that support Adobe PDF. This will allow you to access your book using the latest portable technology any time you want.

Types of Keyboards

There are many types of keyboards you can use to learn. The thing you must know is all the keyboard types have the same keys. You will be able to play all the lesson examples on any of these keyboards. I will tell you about the most common types and how they are different.

Electronic Keyboards

Some of the most common electric keyboards are portable electronic keyboards, electric pianos and synthesizers. The electric keyboard is laid out similar to an acoustic piano and has the same keyboard. But the way an electric keyboard processes sound is different. As an electric instrument, it uses a digital electronic sound module, or tone generator, to produce the sound it needs. Analog or digital technology is used to mimic the half and whole steps with sampled sound.

Electric keyboards come in full-sized 88-key models down to smaller 49-key models. Some are digital, while others are analog circuit based models. Some digital keyboards use prerecorded samples to produce their tone; special algorithms are used to variate the pitch or they are recorded pitch by pitch. Many keyboards offer options for sustain and/or touch response to mimic the feel of a real piano. Some offer full workstation capability for song writing or recording.

Piano

The piano is an acoustic keyboard; it does not require electricity to make sound. There are little hammers inside the piano that strike strings to resonate the notes. Pianos have 88 keys. There are many types of pianos but the most common are the upright, which is classified as a vertical piano, and the grand/baby grand which are horizontal pianos.

Finger Numbers

As you play you will see finger numbers above and below the music. These indicate which finger to use to play that note. Both thumbs are number 1 and both pinkies are number 5.

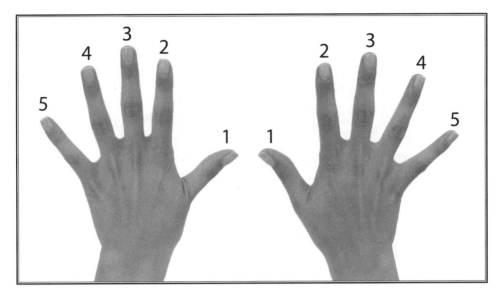

Posture & Hand Placement

You must build great habits right from the beginning. Having proper posture and hand placement will allow you to progress quickly.

Proper Posture

Sit facing the keyboard like the diagram below.

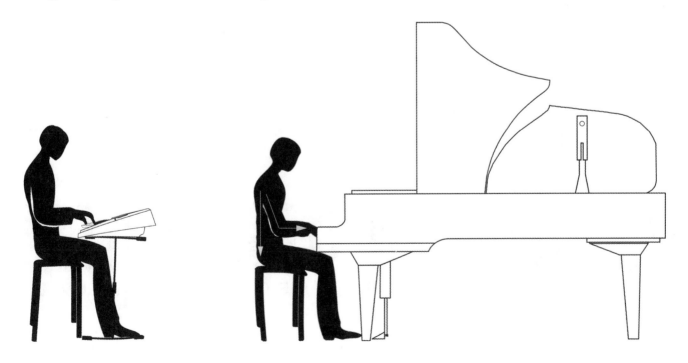

Hand Position

Arch your fingers so that your tips are going straight down in the middle of the keys and curve your thumb inward.

The Musical Alphabet

The musical alphabet consists of seven letters A through G. After G the letters loop back to A and start over again. There are no note names higher in the musical alphabet then G. These seven letters will be the names of the white keys on your keyboard.

A - B - C - D - E - F - G

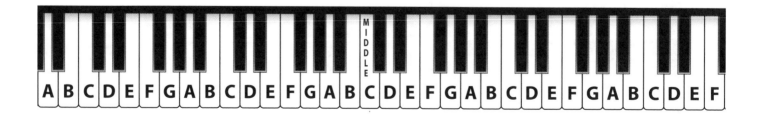

Finding Middle C

Middle C is the note that sits right in the middle of the keyboard and will be a starting point where you divide your left and right hands. You can use the black keys as a guide to find middle C. Locate the two black keys together in the middle of the keyboard, the white key just before the first black key is the middle C note.

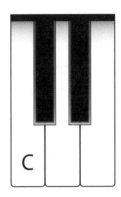

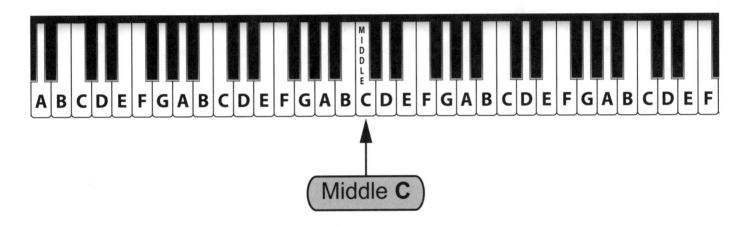

Middle **C**

Right Hand Notes Up from Middle C

Starting with your right hand thumb on the middle C note play five notes up the keyboard. As you play each note say the name out loud.

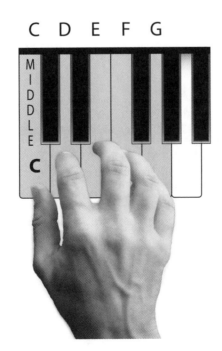

7

The Repeat Sign

A repeat sign (double line with two dots) signifies that all of the written music between the repeat signs is to be repeated.

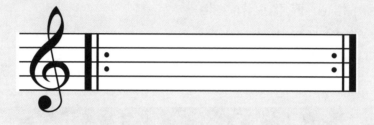

Right Hand Finger Pattern

Here is a right hand pattern to help get your fingers ready to play songs. Make sure to use your finger tips playing one note at a time. Repeat the pattern for five minutes or until your hand gets tired. Practice like this will warm your hand up and build coordination.

$$\| : \quad C - D - E - F - G - F - E - D \quad : \|$$

Finger: 1   2   3   4   5   4   3   2

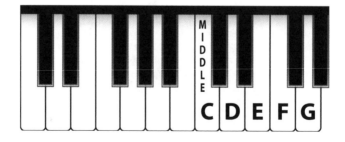

Left Hand Notes Down from Middle C

Starting with your left hand thumb on the middle C note play five notes down the keyboard. Start slow and build up speed gradually.

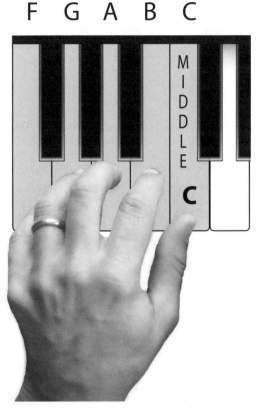

Left Hand Finger Pattern

Here is a left hand pattern to help get your fingers ready to play songs. As you did with your right hand practice this pattern for five minutes a day or until your fingers get tired. As you play say the name of each note out loud. This will help you memorize the notes on your keyboard. Play the notes one at a time using your finger tips.

$$\|: \ C - B - A - G - F - G - A - B \ :\|$$

Finger: 1   2   3   4   5   4   3   2

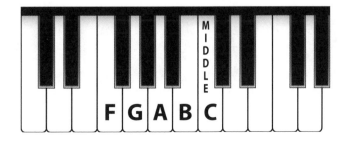

Black Key Groups of Two & Three

The black keys fall into a pattern. There are two together then three together all across the keyboard. This repetitive pattern will help you easily memorize the names of the notes across the keyboard.

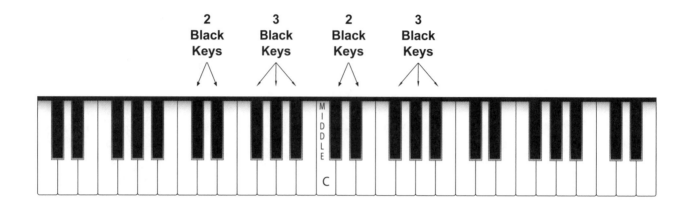

White Key Names Around Two Black Keys

The three white keys around the two black key group are C – D – E. Play these three notes across the keyboard.

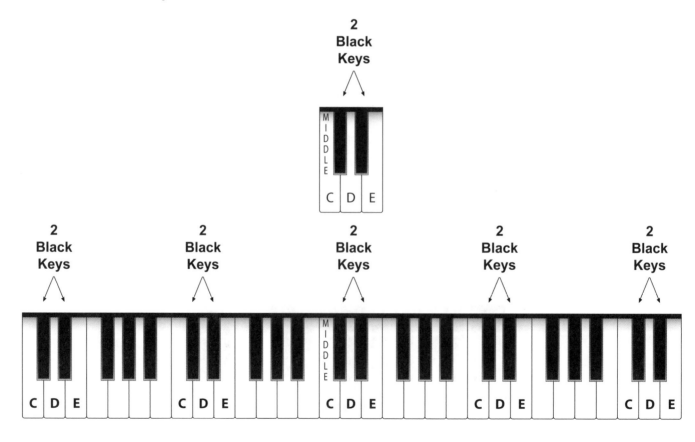

White Key Names Around Three Black Keys

The four white keys around the three black key group are F - G - A - B. Play these four notes across the keyboard. Memorize the note locations. This will help you as you learn songs.

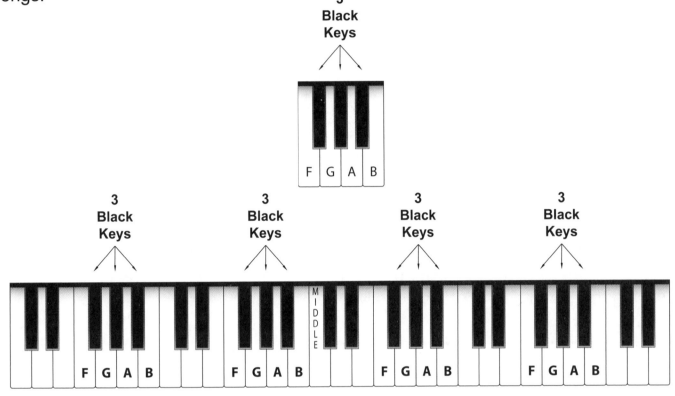

Locating Notes Across the Keyboard

Use the black keys as a guide to locate notes across the keyboard. Play each of the following notes across your keyboard and call out it's name.

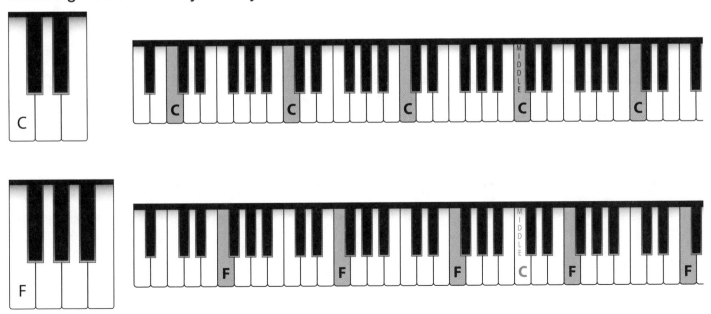

Treble Staff

Music is written on a **STAFF** consisting of **FIVE LINES** and **FOUR SPACES**. The lines and spaces are numbered as shown:

5th Line	
	4th Space
4th Line	
	3rd Space
3rd Line	
	2nd Space
2nd Line	
	1st Space
1st Line	

The lines and spaces are named after letters of the alphabet. You can use the saying to memorize the names easily. The lines are named as follows:

5	(F)	Fine
4	(D)	Does
3	(B)	Boy
2	(G)	Good
1	(E)	Every

The letter names of the spaces are F - A - C - E they spell the word "FACE."

4	E
3	C
2	A
1	F

F-A-C-E

Staff Symbols

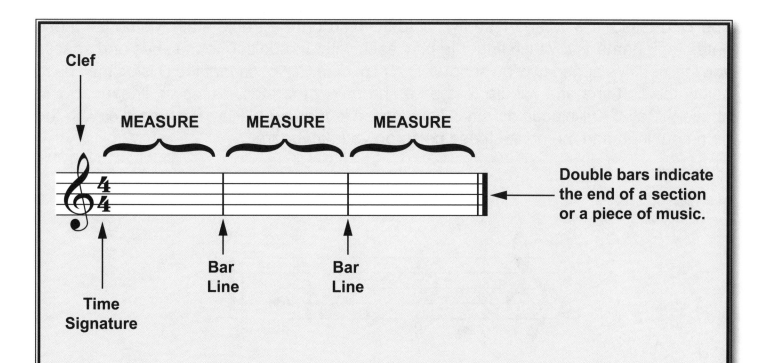

Measures & Bar Lines

The staff is divided into measures by vertical lines called bar lines.

Treble Clef

The second line of the treble clef is known as the G line. Some people call the treble clef the "G clef" because the tail circles around the G line of the staff.

Time Signature

Time signatures are written at the beginning of a piece of music. The top number tells you how many beats there are in each measure and the bottom number tells what type of beat is receiving the count.

Learn Piano 1 - Quiz 1

Once you complete this section go to RockHouseMethod.com and take the quiz to track your progress. You will receive an email with your results and suggestions.

Right Hand Notes on the Treble Staff

The next lessons will use these five notes played on the treble staff. Memorize these notes their name and which finger to play each with. In addition to the lines and spaces you learned I've added two lower notes D and middle C. Notice that the D is on the space below the first line and middle C is on a line below the staff. Notes on lines below or above the staff are placed on small lines called ledger lines. Play each note saying the name out loud and memorize these notes on your keyboard.

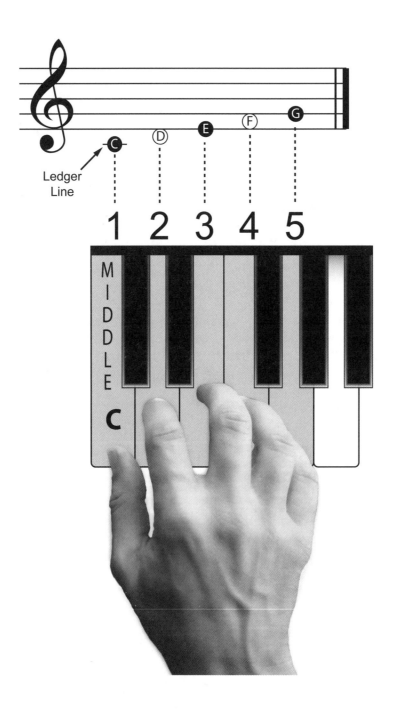

Note Values - Quarter, Half & Whole Notes

Notes will tell you how long each note rings. Below are the first note types you will be using in this book. Play the examples for each note type below. Make sure to hold your finger pressed down on each note for the entire duration.

Whole Note = 4 Beats

A whole note has a hollow head and no stem and receives four beats or counts.

Count: 1   2   3   4

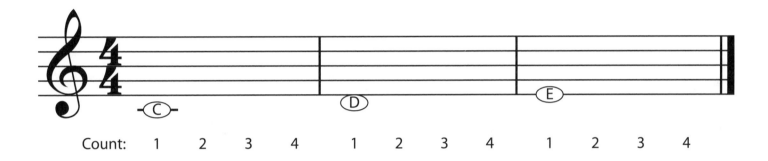

Count: 1   2   3   4   1   2   3   4   1   2   3   4

Half Note = 2 Beats

A half note has a hollow head and a stem and receives two beats, or counts.

Count: 1   2   3   4

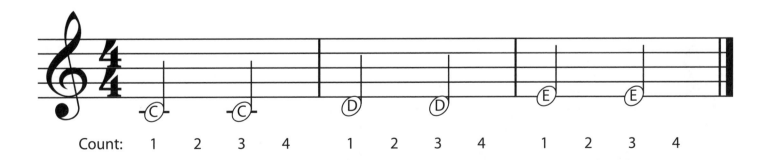

Count: 1   2   3   4   1   2   3   4   1   2   3   4

Quarter Note = 1 Beat

A quarter note has a solid head and a stem and receives one beat, or count.

Count: 1   2   3   4

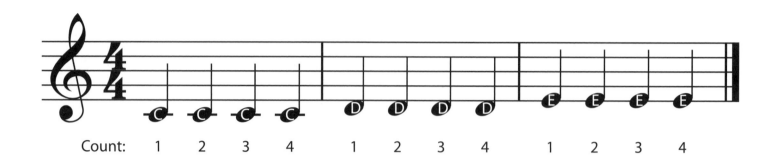

Count: 1   2   3   4   1   2   3   4   1   2   3   4

Hot Cross Buns

As you practice this song pay attention to the timing and how long to let each note ring. You can count along as you play 1 - 2 - 3 - 4 for each measure. Start to memorize each notes location on the staff.

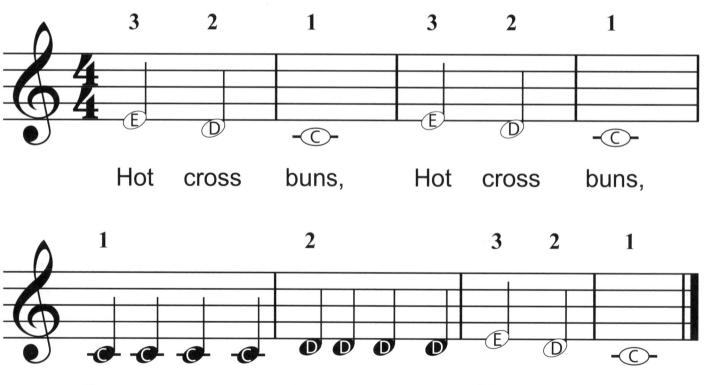

By the Silv'ery Moonlight

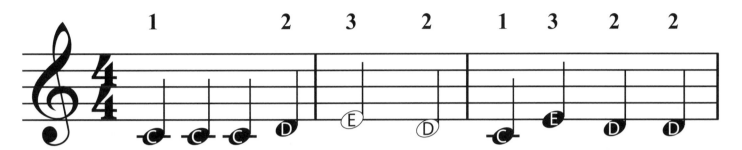

By the sil-v'ry moon-light,   my dear friend Pier-

rot,   May I have your   pen   to

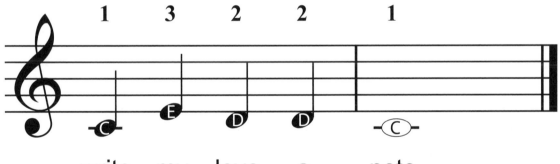

write my love a   note.

Backing Tracks

Many of the songs songs in this book will have a backing track that you can play along with. These will be either audio demonstrations or full band tracks. This will help you learn to play with other musicians. The songs with backing tracks will be depicted with the CD track icon.

Rain Rain Go Away

You will now play the F and G notes. Make sure to use the proper finger to play each note.

Rain,   rain,   Go   a - way.

Come   a - gain some   o - ther   day

Key Dynamics

Dynamics in music is the difference between loud and soft. Many keyboards are dynamic and notes can be played louder or softer. On a piano the keys are velocity sensitive, this means the harder you hit the note the louder it will sound. Some electronic keyboards have touch sensitive keys as well but many electronic keyboards are not dynamic.

Go Tell Aunt Rhody

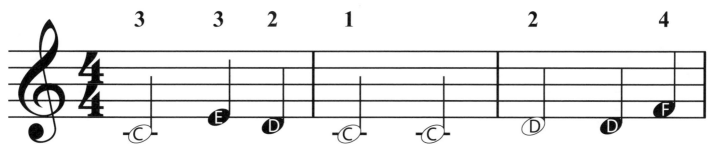

Go   tell   Aunt   Rho – dy,   Go   tell   Aunt

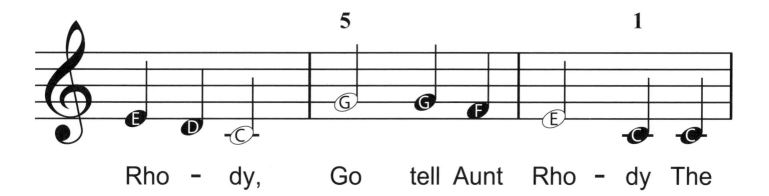

Rho – dy,   Go   tell   Aunt   Rho – dy   The

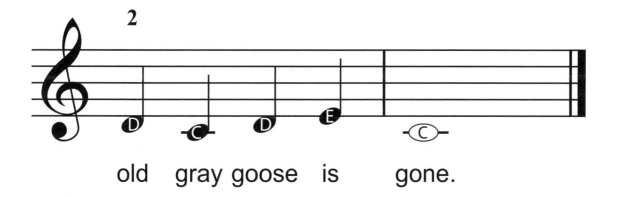

old   gray   goose   is   gone.

The next songs will not have the letters inside the notes. As you play call the note names out loud to help memorize the notes. You must now learn the notes by location on the staff. Middle C is always on the line below the staff, D the space below the staff and E is on the bottom line.

19

Aura Lee

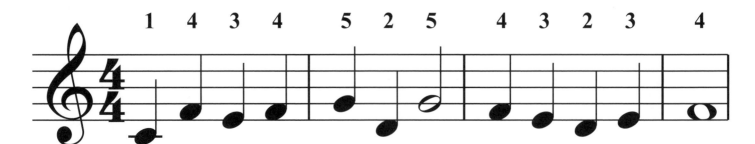

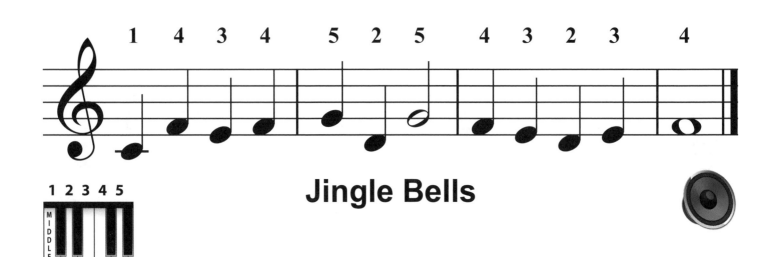

Jingle Bells

Jin - gle bells!   Jin - gle bells jin - gle   all   the   way!

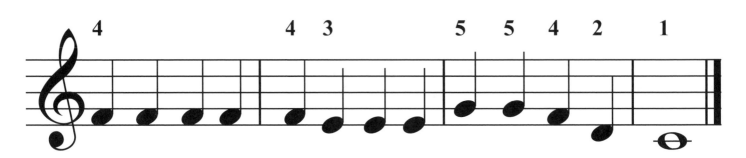

Oh what fun it   is   to   ride a   one horse o - pen   sleigh!

Good King Wenceslas

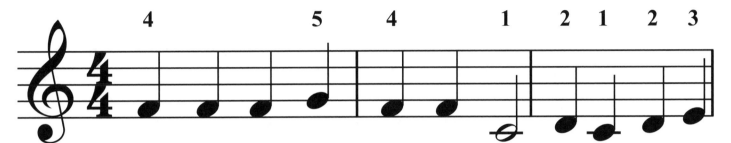

Good King Wen ces - las looked out, On the feast of

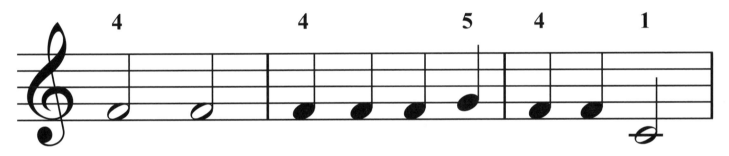

Ste - phen   When the snow lay   round a - bout,

Deep and crisp and   e - ven.

Metronome

A metronome is a device that clicks at an adjustable rate that you set. It is used to help develop a sense of timing and to help gauge your progress.
By playing along with the clicking sound you get the sense of playing with another musician. Each click represents one beat; a common way to count beats is to tap your foot. One beat would equal tapping your foot down up. Play all the songs and exercises in this book along with a metronome. If you don't have a metronome you can download one for free at the lesson support site.

White Key Finger Flexing

Now let's get your fingers moving on the keyboard. The following are a series of warm up exercises to get your fingers coordinated and ready to play more complicated music. The numbers represent the finger you will use to play each note. Look at the diagram to see which key each finger aligns with. Just like athletes warm up before games musicians should warm up before playing for peak performance.

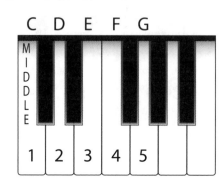

Right Hand

Example 1

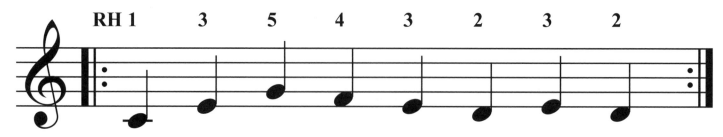

Example 2

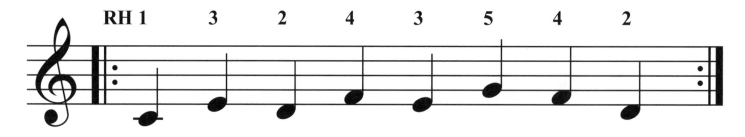

Pick Up Notes

When there is an incomplete measure starting a song these notes are called "pick up notes." When this occurs the last measure will also be incomplete; but, the combination of both together will equal a full measure. When counting into the song still count the full count but just start later.

A Tisket, a Tasket

A tis - ket, a tas - ket, a green and yel - low bas - ket, I

wrote a let - ter to my love, and on the way I dropped it.

Dotted Half Notes

A dotted half note receives three beats or counts. It is a regular half note with a dot placed after it.

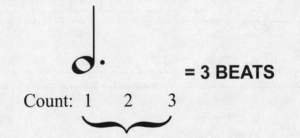

= 3 BEATS

Count: 1   2   3

3/4 Timing

Here is a new time signature that will be used in the next song. In 3/4 time there is three beats per measure. This timing is used in many pieces.

I Saw Three Ships

Count: 1 2 3

I   saw   three   ships   come   sail - ing   in,   On

Christ - mas   Day   On   Christ - mas   Day,   I

saw   three   ships   come   sail - ing   in,   On

Christ - mas   Day   in   the   morn - ing.

Rests

The next melody contains your first rests. A rests is a period of silence. Like whole, half and quarter notes you keep time only there is no sound. See what each rest looks like below.

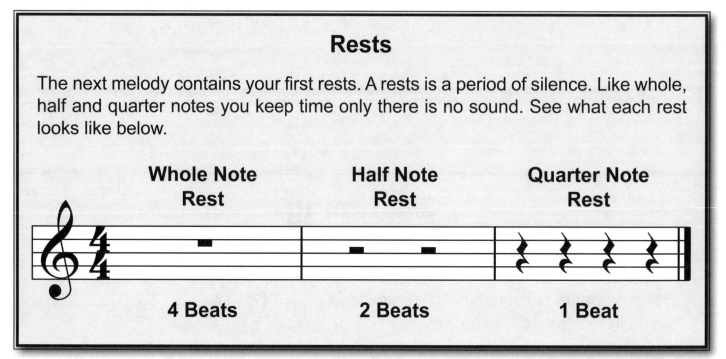

Whole Note Rest	Half Note Rest	Quarter Note Rest
4 Beats	2 Beats	1 Beat

Oh, When the Saints

Oh, when the saints,   Go march-ing in.

Oh, when the saints go march - ing in.

Oh, Lord I want to be in that numb - er.

When the saints go march - ing in.

Dynamics in Music

As you are playing a song there will often be symbols that tell you what dynamic level to play the song. The dynamic level is how loud or soft the song should be played. The following are common symbols used for dynamics.

p - Piano, meaning soft

mp - Mezzo-piano, meaning medium soft

mf - Mezzo-forte, meaning medium loud

f - Forte, meaning loud

25

Fais Dodo

Go to sleep, my Cal - vin my bro - ther,

Go to sleep, you'll soon have some sweets. Our

mo - ther's up - stairs, She'll bake us a cake, Our

fa - ther's down - stairs, Some cho - c'late he'll make.

Go to sleep my Cal - vin my bro - ther,

Go to sleep, you'll soon have some sweets.

Away in the Forest

Count: 1 2 3 4

A - way in the deep fo - rest, The o - wl hoots,"Yoo - hoo." While

from a grand old oak tree Re - plies the small cuc - koo: "Cuc -

koo, cuc - koo", Re - plies the small cuc - koo. "Cuc -

koo, cuc - koo", Re - plies the small cuc - koo.

The Tie

When notes on the **same** line or space are joined with a curved line, they are called tied notes. The note is only played once but will ring for the combined values of both notes.

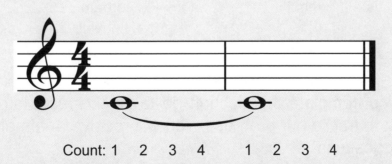

Count: 1 2 3 4 1 2 3 4

Left Hand Cross Over

At times you will need to cross your left hand over the right hand to play notes in order to make the song flow smoothly. I've outlined the three notes in the following song in which you will cross over and play with your left hand 2nd finger.

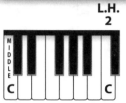

Row, Row, Row your Boat

Row, row, row your boat,

Gent - ly down the stream,_____

Mer - ri - ly mer - ri - ly, mer - ri - ly, mer - ri - ly,

Life is but a dream._____

Learn Piano 1 - Quiz 2

Once you complete this section go to RockHouseMethod.com and take the quiz to track your progress. You will receive an email with your results and suggestions.

Bass Staff

← The bass clef is used for music to be played with the left hand. It is also called the F clef because it circles around the F line.

This staff also has five lines and four spaces but the names will be different then the treble clef. he lines on the staff are G – B – D – F – A. A saying that will help you memorize these lines are Good – Boys – Do – Fine – Always. Look below at all the notes across the bass staff.

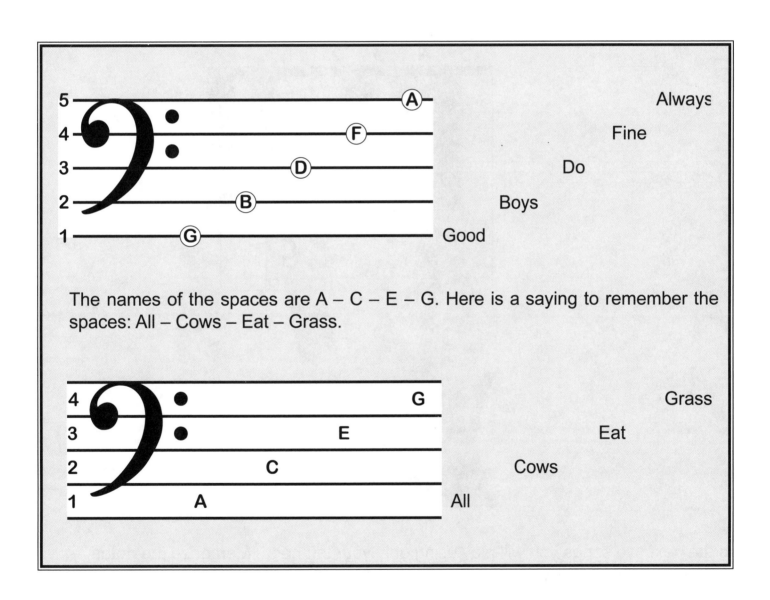

The names of the spaces are A – C – E – G. Here is a saying to remember the spaces: All – Cows – Eat – Grass.

Left Hand Notes on the Bass Staff

The next lessons will use these five notes played on the treble staff. Memorize these notes their name and which finger to play each with.

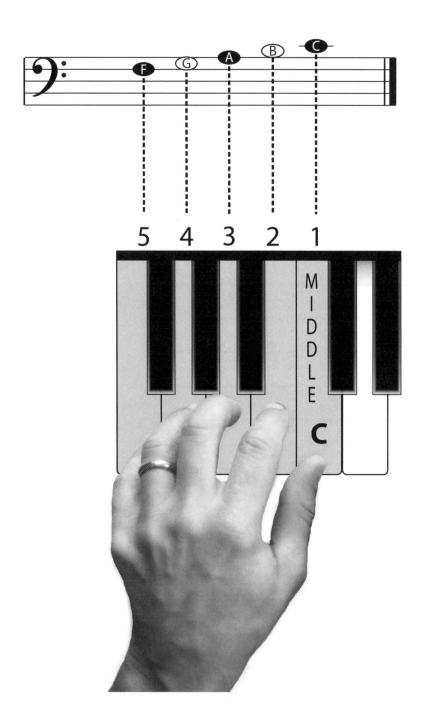

In the next two songs you will play using only your left hand. Memorize the notes because you will combine both hands playing songs soon.

Lefty Lucy

Move to the Left

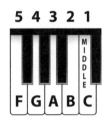

Left Hand Finger Flexing

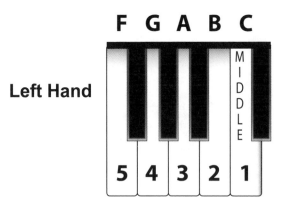

Example 1

Example 2

The Grand Staff

Piano music is written on a grand staff. This staff combines the treble and bass staffs together. They are connected by bar lines and a brace.

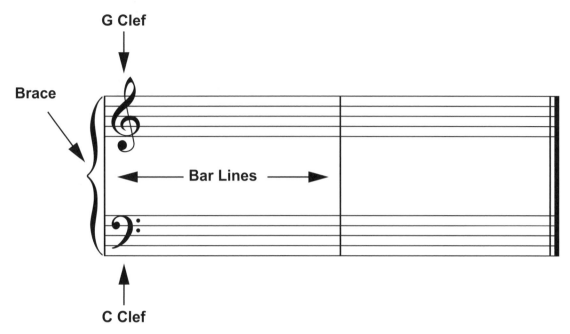

Below are the notes on the grand staff. Use the diagram so you can see where they fall on your keyboard.

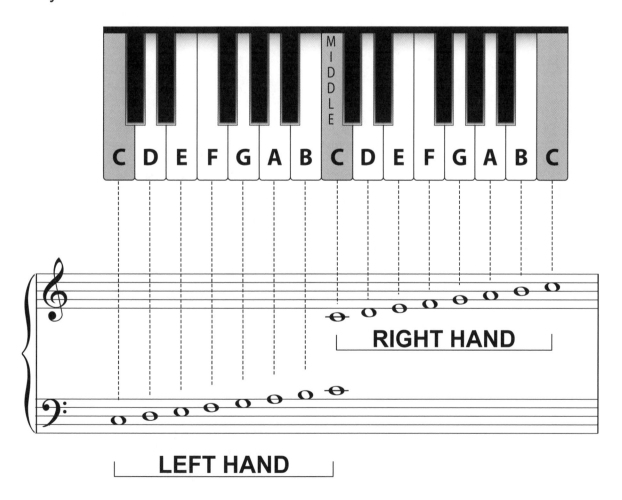

Two Thumbs on C

Now you will play using both hands together. Look below to see the proper way to place your hands on the keyboard.

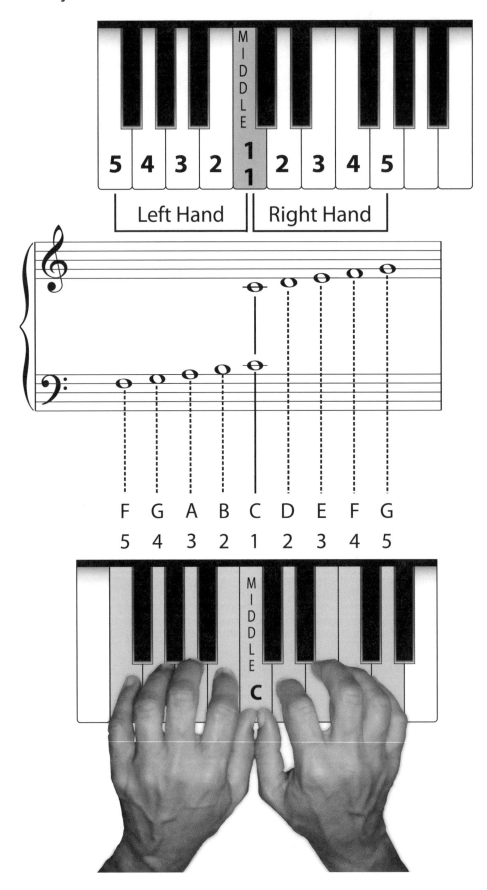

Reading Two Staffs

Now you will be reading two staffs together. The bottom bass staff will be played with your left hand and the top treble staff will be played with your right hand. It will take time and practice to read music this way so be patient. Start each song at a slow pace and build speed gradually.

Yankee Doodle

Here is your first song playing notes with both hands. Take your time and pay attention to the finger numbers to make this song easier to play. The fingers on both hands should always be on the keys in position to play notes.

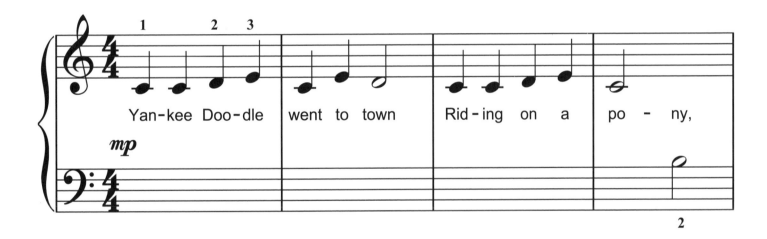

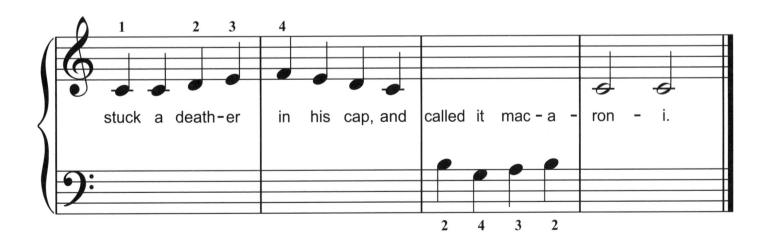

London Bridge

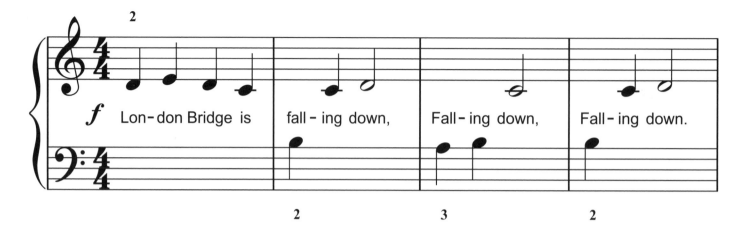

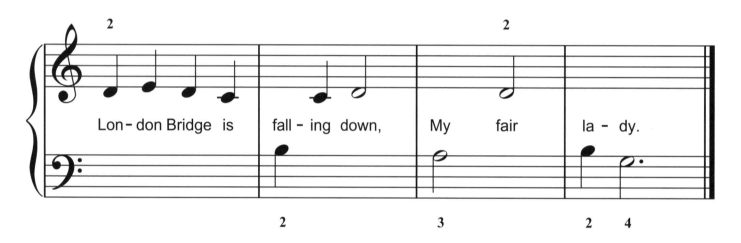

Tempo

Tempo is the speed in which music is played. It is measured in beats per minute or bpm. There will be tempo setting at the beginning of many songs that require a specific tempo. Here are some of the most common tempo settings.

Adagio - Slow - 66 - 76 bpm

Andante - Moderately Slow - 76 - 108 bpm

Moderato - Moderate - 108 - 120 bpm

Allegro - Fast - 120 - 168 bpm

Twinkle Twinkle Little Star

Andante

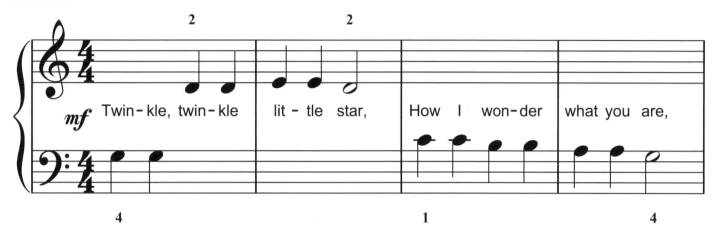

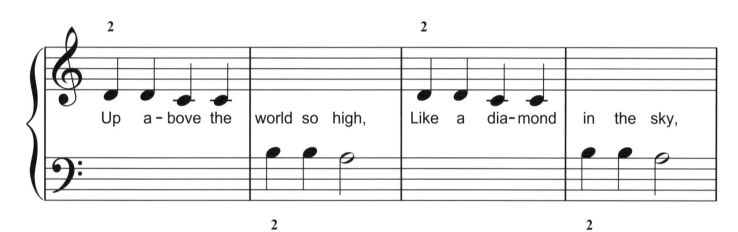

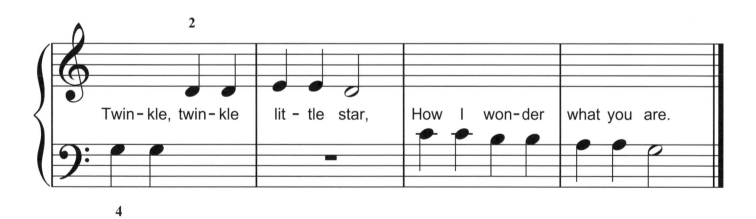

Jolly Old Saint Nicholas

Moderato

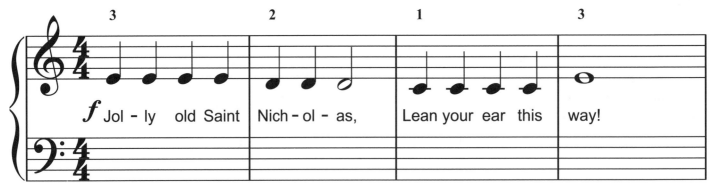

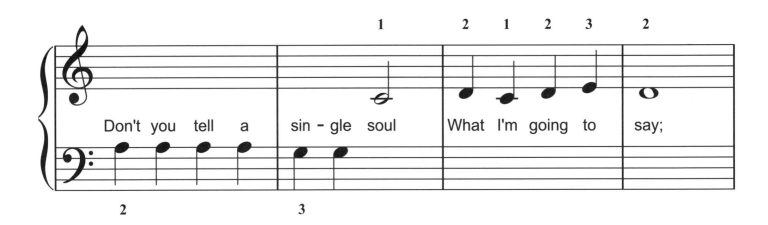

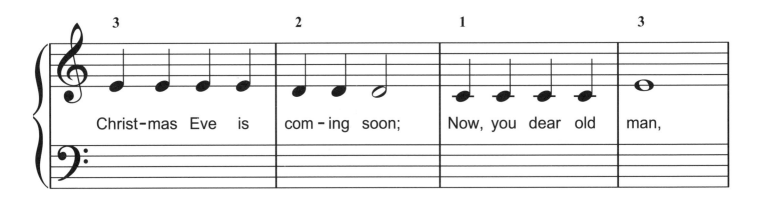

Camptown Races

Moderato

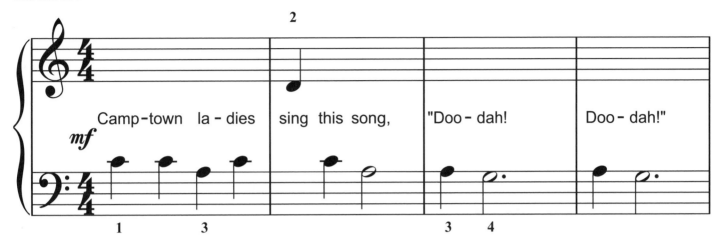

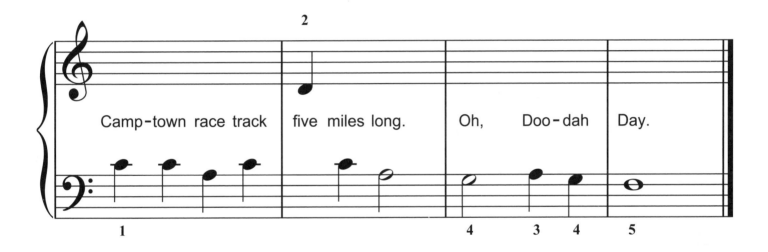

Ritardando

Ritardando (or rit.) is a musical term that means a section of music is to gradually slow down. It is written in music with the letters rit. followed by dashed horizontal line indicating the length. This can add emotion to a song.

Two Hands Together

From this point on the songs will require you to play notes with both hands together at times. This requires practice and concentration. You should isolate any sections that you have difficulty with and practice them repetitively. "Repetition is the mother of skill"

Bingo

The last two measures of this song have a ritardando. Slow the tempo down to make a dramatic ending.

Moderato

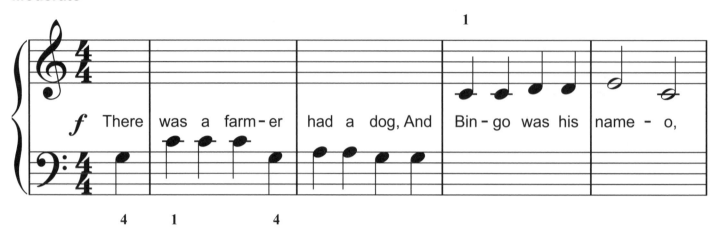

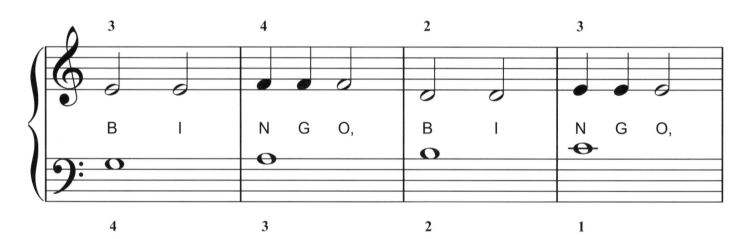

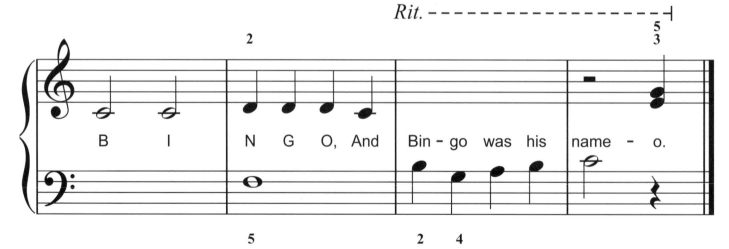

40

We Three Kings

Andante

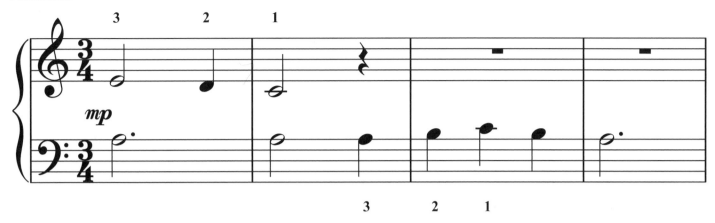

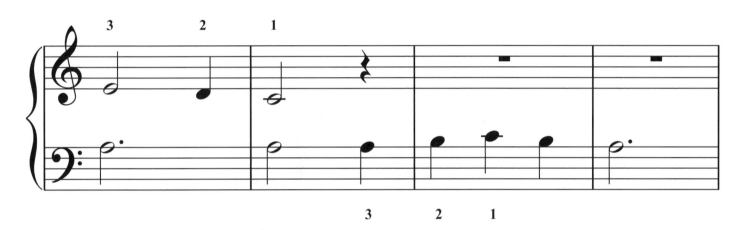

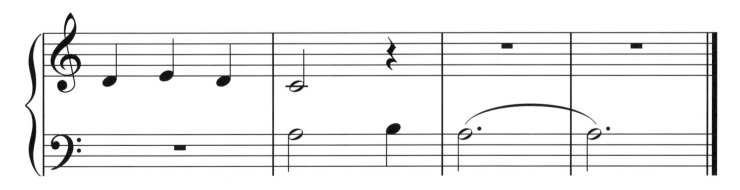

Left Hand C Position Notes

Here are the left hand C position notes on the bass staff. Play through these notes and memorize them. You will be combining both hands to play in C position in the coming lessons.

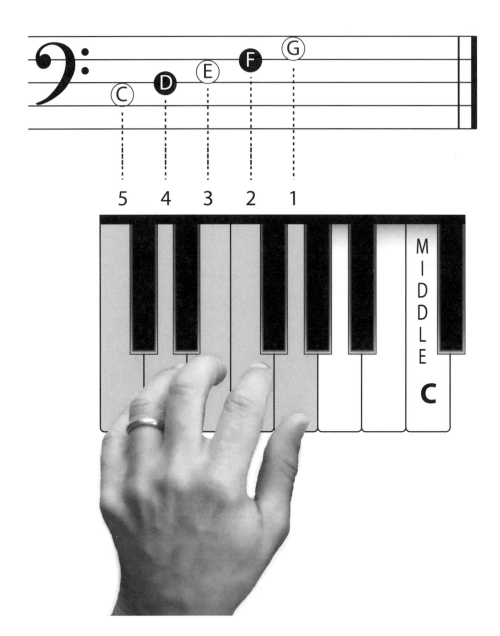

The next two songs you will play using only your left hand in C position. Memorize where the notes are on the staff and their names. Say the name of each note out loud as you play to help learn effectively.

Aura Lee

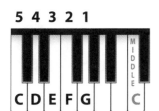

Ode To Joy

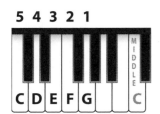

C Position Both Hands

The next lessons will contain music written in what's called "C Position." This is a starting point that you will place both hands on the keyboard to play the music effectively. There will be some notes outside this region that you will need to play as well. Below are the C position notes on the grand staff. Use the diagram so you can see where they fall on your keyboard. Play them and call the note names out loud.

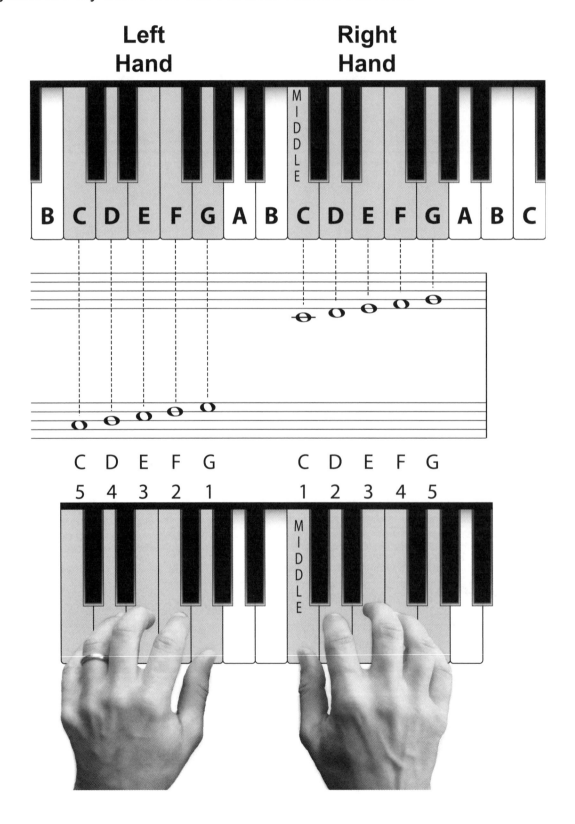

Etude with Two Hands

The following songs will be played in C position using both hands. Pay close attention to the fingering there will be some notes that will be played extending the position notes. This C hand position is just a starting point to give you a base but as you progress you will expand your note knowledge to play the entire keyboard.

Andante

Expanding Your Note Reach

In the next song your left hand will play notes from C up to A. Position your left hand one key higher then the C position so your 1st finger can play the A note. You will shift back down to C position to play the last note C. In the coming songs you will also expand to play more notes with your right hand. Pay close attention to the fingering.

Old MacDonald

Run Away Train

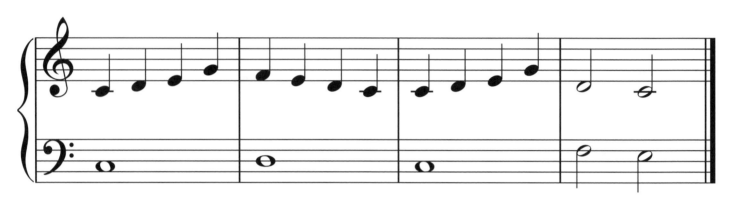

Bottoms Up

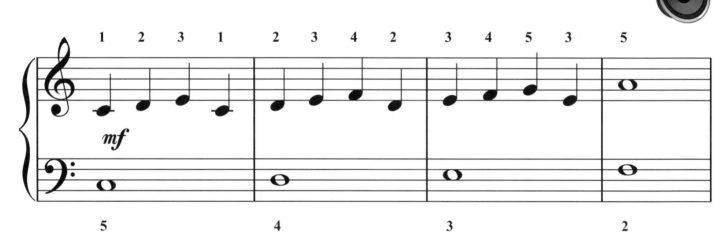

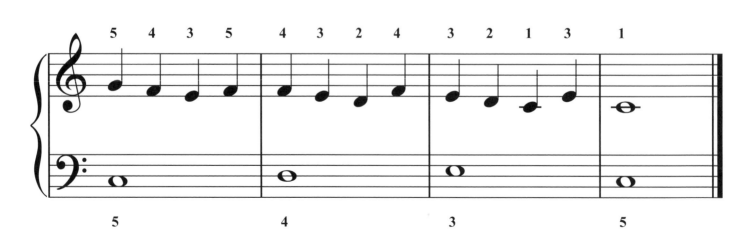

48

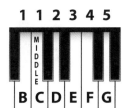

Surprise Symphony

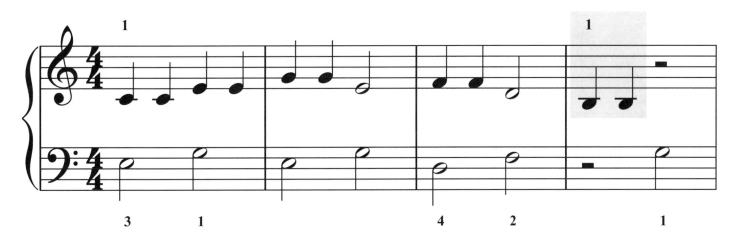

Practice Tips

- Make sure to review previous lessons. A good idea is to review the past songs as a warm up before you start your new lesson.

- Use a metronome when practicing. Always start at a slow speed and increase your tempo once you can play the speed you are at comfortably.

- Record yourself if you have the capacity. When you listen back you will be more objective to any inconsistencies. Learn to be your own biggest critic.

Oh, When the Saints

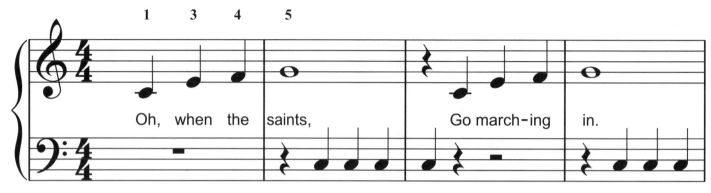

Oh, when the saints, Go march-ing in.

Count: 1 2 3 4 - 1 **2** **3** **4** 5

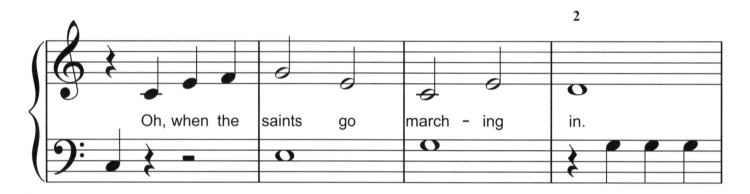

Oh, when the saints go march - ing in.

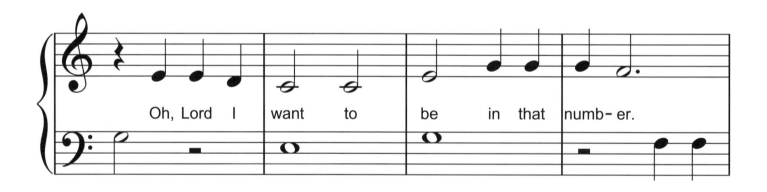

Oh, Lord I want to be in that numb- er.

When the saints go march - ing in.

Congratulations you've made it to the end of Book 1! Go to RockHouseMethod.com and take the quiz to track your progress. You will receive an email with your results and an official Rock House Method "Certificate of Completion" when you pass.

You have complete Piano Level 1

You can go to RockHouseMethod.com and download a Certificate of Completion. You are now ready to begin Rock House Level 2.

KEY TAB SECTION

As you start level 2 you can also start the Rock House exclusive "Key Tab" section starting on page 144. In this section you will learn chords, chord progressions and many piano riffs to make your learning fun and exciting.

Book 2 Table of Contents

Words from the Author

To learn a new language you take small steps, progressively increasing your knowledge until you speak it fluidly. Music is the language you are learning. With consistent practice this book will take you to the next level, attaining your goal to play music. In this book you will learn the important basics to build a solid foundation of music. Don't just play; take time to listen to what you are playing as well as other musicians. When your ears hear and understand music, your fingers will respond. So let's get to our pianos, open our ears and mind and play music

John McCarthy

Johnny Blues Man

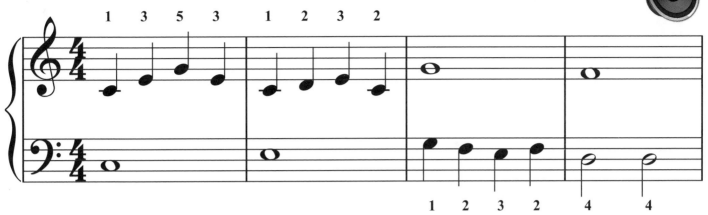

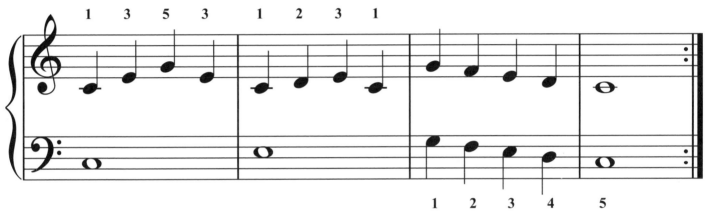

A Day at the Beach

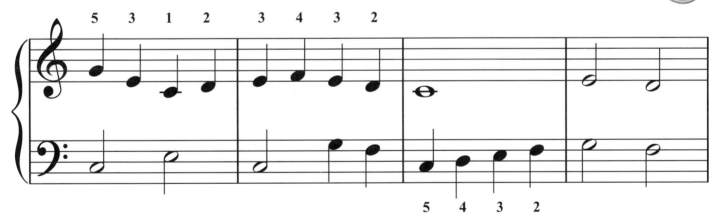

Purple Phraze

Amanda Lynn

54

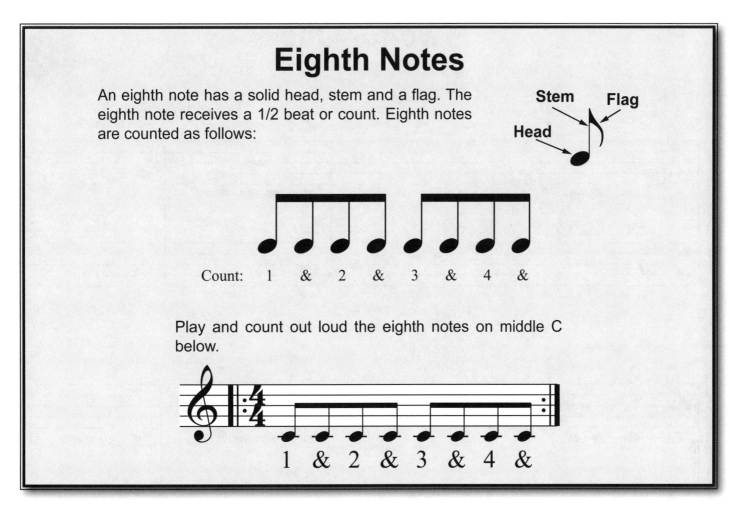

The Rhythm Pyramid

The following diagram breaks down the note values you have learned. This diagram is known as the rhythm pyramid. At the top of the pyramid is the whole note which receives four beats, as you travel towards the bottom of the pyramid the note division keeps dividing in half. For example, the whole note is divided in half and becomes two half notes receiving two beats each, then half note divides into two equal parts of one beat each, 2 quarter notes, etc.

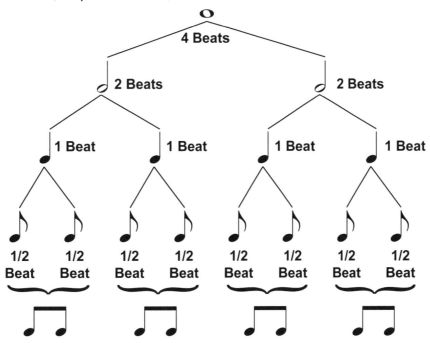

Two for One

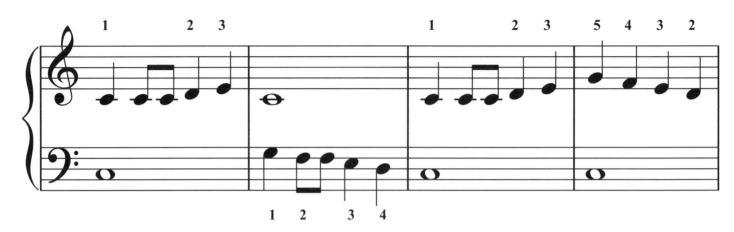

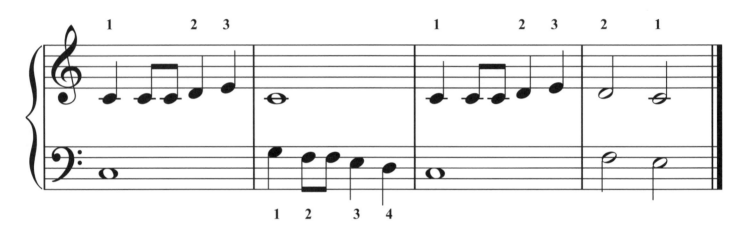

The Arkansas Traveler

Be sure to take notice that this song is played with the "Two Thumbs on C" hand positioning.

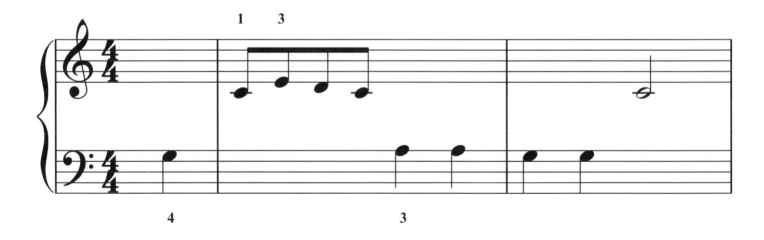

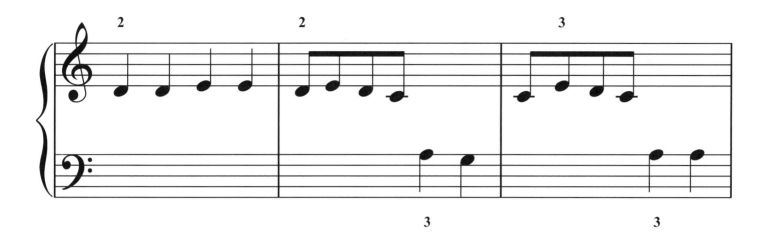

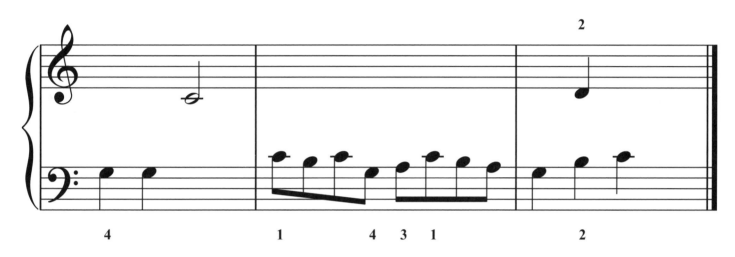

Dotted Quarter Notes

A dotted quarter note has a solid head with a dot next to it and a stem. The dotted quarter note receives 1 1/2 beats (counts).

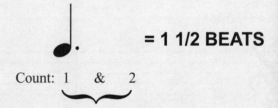

= 1 1/2 BEATS

Count: 1 & 2

Dotted quarter notes are often followed by eighth notes to make an even two beats. Below are a series of dotted quarter and eighth notes on middle C. Play and count these out loud.

1 & 2 & 3 & 4 & 1 & 2 & 3 & 4 &

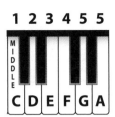

Kum-Ba-Ya

In this song you will extend your right hand notes to play an A note. See where this A note is on the keyboard diagram. You will play both the G and A notes with your right hand 5th finger.

Moderato

African Folk Hymn

Kum-Ba - Ya my Lord,   Kum-Ba - Ya.   Kum-Ba -

Ya   my Lord,   Kum - Ba - Ya.   Kum - Ba -

Ya   my Lord,   Kum - Ba - Ya.   Oh

Lord,   Kum - Ba - Ya.

Half Steps

An interval is the distance between two notes. The smallest interval in music is the half step. A half step would be the distance from any key to the very next key. If you play any note and then play the next key you are playing a half step.

The New Years Song

Sometimes when playing a song you will have to use one finger for two keys to expand the range. In this song you will use this technique with both hands. In measure two, finger one will play the C and B notes. In measure five, you play the A note with your right hand fifth finger. In the eighth measure you will play the G and the A notes with your left hand first finger. See where these sections are noted within the song in grey and pay close attention to the fingering.

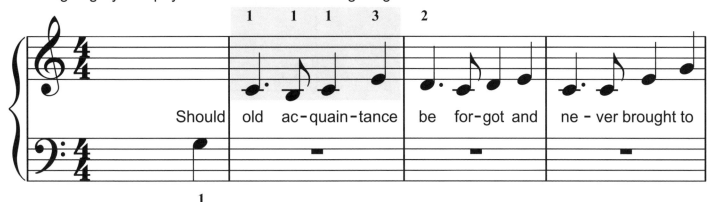

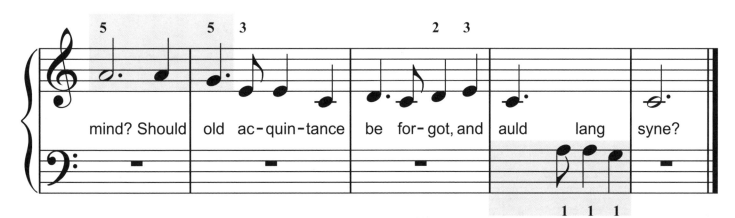

Sharps & Flats

A sharp raises a note a half step (one key) and a flat lowers a note a half step (one key). The black keys on your keyboard are the sharp and flat notes. Each black key will have two names.

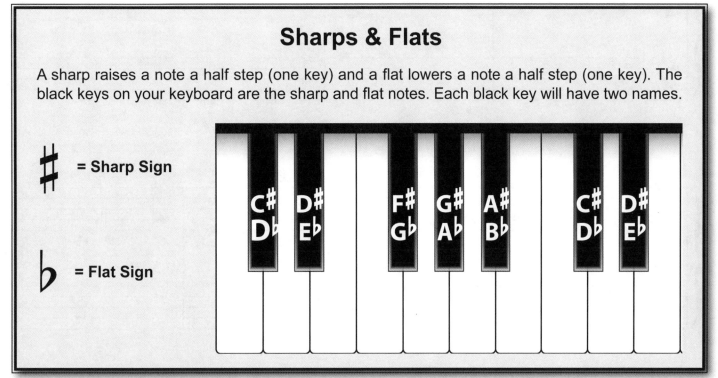

Ode to Joy

Ludwig Van Beethoven

Staccato

Staccato is a small dot placed on top or bottom of a note that indicates that you cut the note short and detached not letting it ring out.

Turkey in the Straw

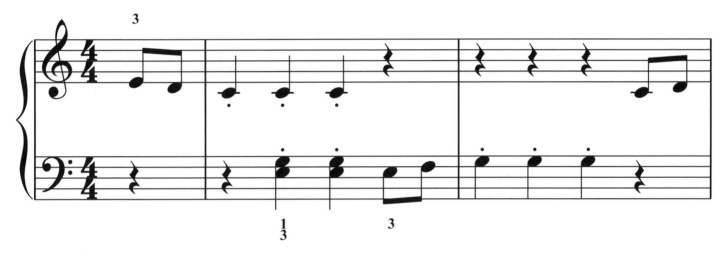

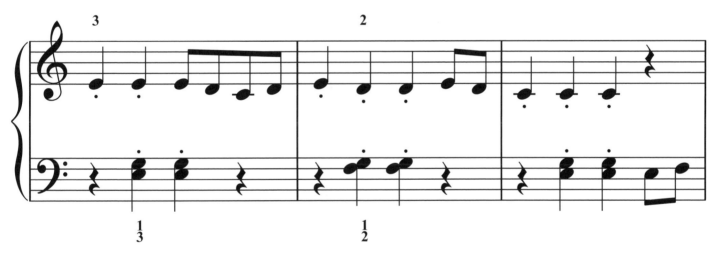

Row, Row, Row Your Boat

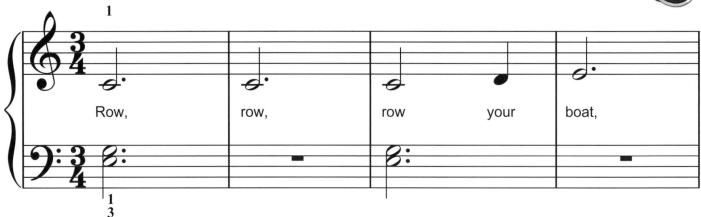

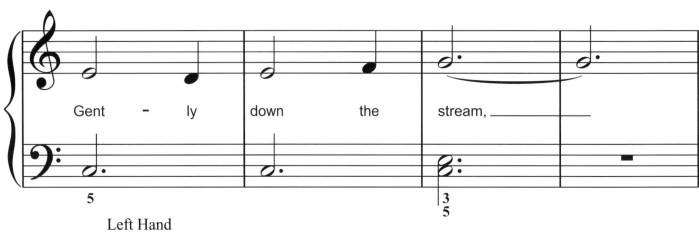

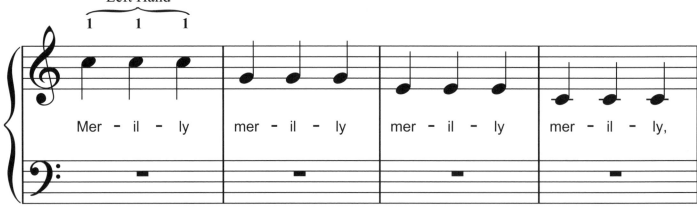

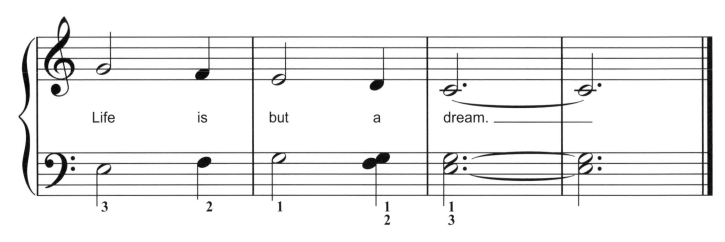

Bridal March

In this song there will be two right hand variations. In measure two you will shift down to play the B and C with your first and second fingers. In measure four there is a right hand cross over. To play the B note cross your second finger over your first finger to play that note then swing it back to play the D note. I have depicted these notes with circles around the finger number.

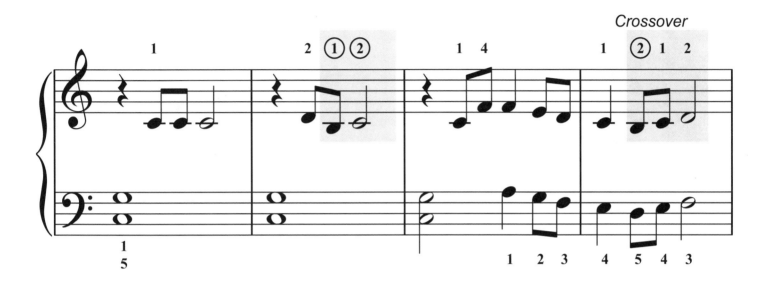

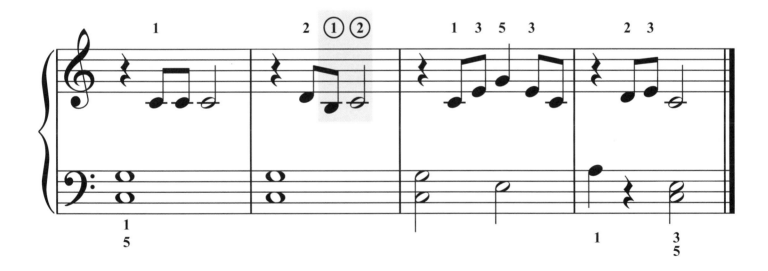

Learn Piano 2 - Quiz 1
Once you complete this section go to RockHouseMethod.com and take the quiz to track your progress. You will receive an email with your results and suggestions.

Your First Chords
C Major

A chord is three or more notes sounded together. A major chord has a happy, bright sound. There is an easy way to form a major chord which I call the 4-3 method. By counting up four keys, then three keys, from any note you form a major chord. This is also four half steps and three half steps. Let's form a C major chord:

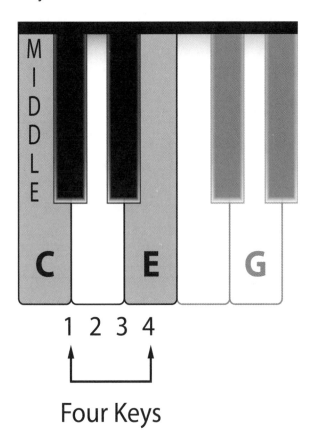

Four Keys

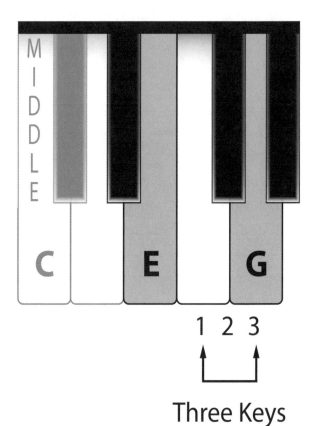

Three Keys

Start with the middle C note (the starting note is the root note, or name, of the chord), count up four keys (both black and white) this is the E note.

Next count up three keys, this is the G note.

The C major chord contains the notes C – E – G played together. Make sure to use the proper fingers to play the chord most effectively.

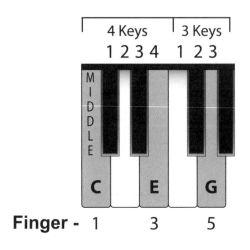

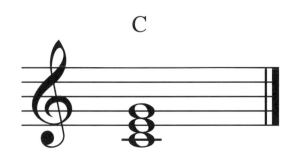

F Major

Now use the same method to form an F major chord. Start with the F note and go four keys up, this is the A note. Next go up three keys, this is the C note. The F major chord contains the notes F – A – C played together. Again, make sure to use the proper fingers to play each note.

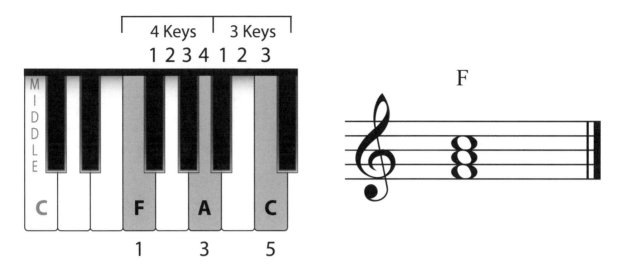

Playing Chords Across the Keyboard

You can play these two chords anywhere on the piano's keyboard. Play each chord starting with the lowest notes up to the highest. The keyboard diagrams below show where these chords are found across the piano.

C Major

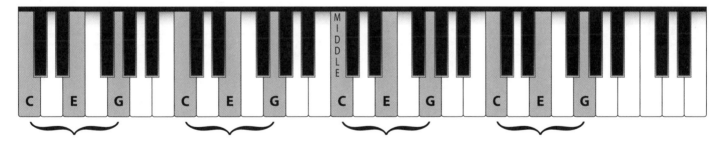

F Major

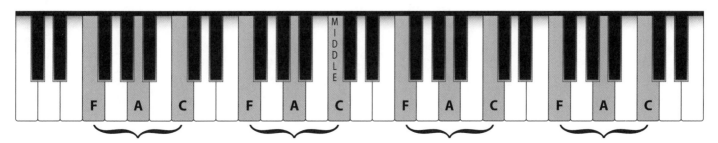

Your First Chord Progression

Now you will play the C and F major chords and form your first chord progression. Play each chord two times in whole note timing. Play the chord progression below along with the backing track and hear how it makes a complete song.

You can play the same chord progression with half and quarter note timing. Play the progressions below. You can also play these variations along with the same backing track.

Half Notes

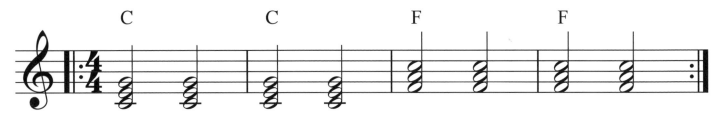

Quarter Notes

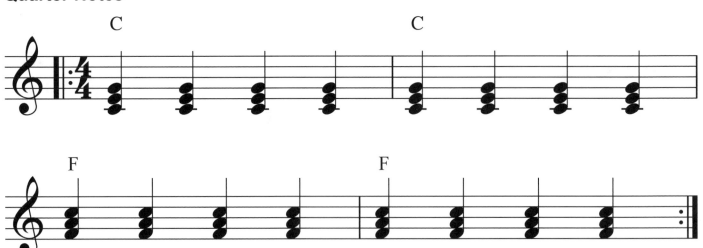

Sustain & Damper Pedal

Most pianos come with two or three pedals. The pedal on the far right is called the *damper* pedal. Many times this pedal is also called a sustain pedal. When the pedal is pressed it "turns on" the sustained effect by lifting the dampers off of the piano strings which allows the notes to ring even after you have lifted your fingers away from the keys. If you are using an electric keyboard most have an input for a sustain pedal to plug in on the back.

There are very specific symbols used in classical music indicating when to press the sustain pedal and when the sustain should be off completely. The symbols look like this:

$\mathcal{Ped}.$ - Press down or change damper (sustain) pedal.

✻ - Completely remove damper (sustain) pedal.

Below is an example of using the damper pedal in a musical context:

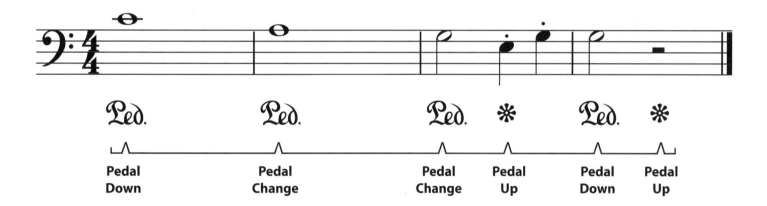

One last thing I want to mention; sometimes in popular music arrangements specific pedal symbols are not used. Instead, the words "with pedal" might be seen under the first measure. And in other cases there is no mention of the pedal leaving the usage of the pedal up to the performer. Use your discretion as well as your ears and you will always sound great when you play!

Single Note Exercises

It is important to get your hands coordinated so you can play complicated pieces with ease. The following exercises will challenge your right and left hands. Take your time starting slowly then build your speed up gradually. I recommend that you use a metronome to help gauge your progress.

Example 1: Right Hand Ascending

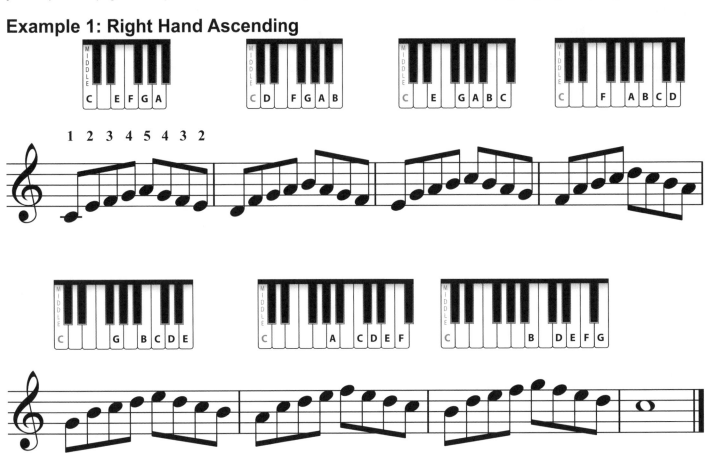

Right Hand Descending

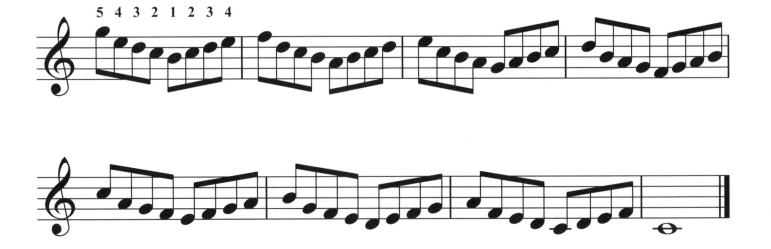

Example 2: Left Hand Ascending

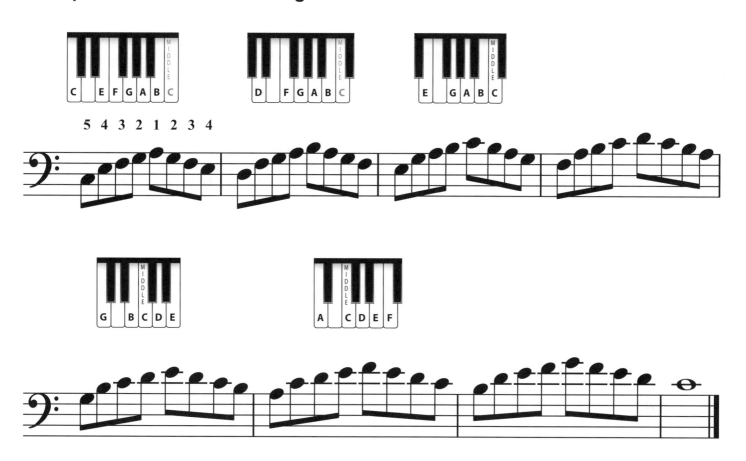

Left Hand Descending

Example 3: Both Hands Ascending

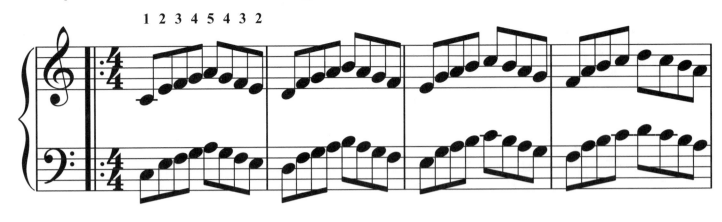

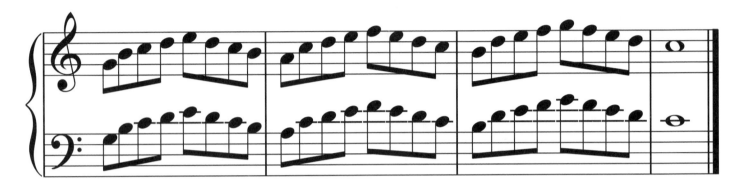

Both Hands Descending

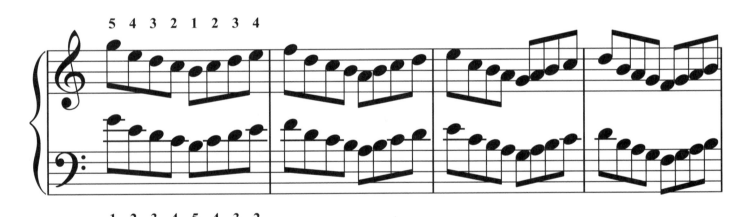

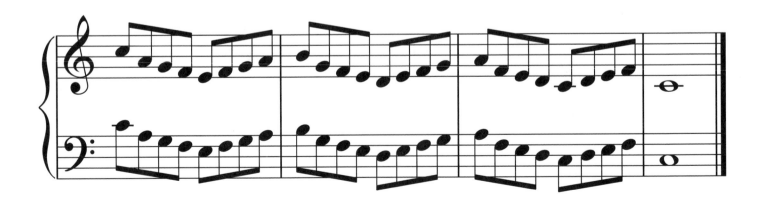

Intervals – Whole & Half Steps

As you learned earlier, if you play any note and then play the next key you are playing a half step. There are two natural half steps that are B to C and E to F. These are two white keys in a row. A whole step is made up of two half steps.

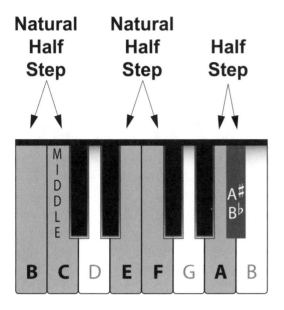

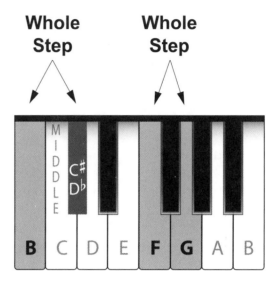

Writing Half & Whole Steps

Now that you have learned what a half and whole step are on the keyboard write a series of half and whole steps on the keyboard diagrams below. Write the letter name of the two notes directly on the key and over the diagram write an H or W for whole or half step. I've done a few to help you get started:

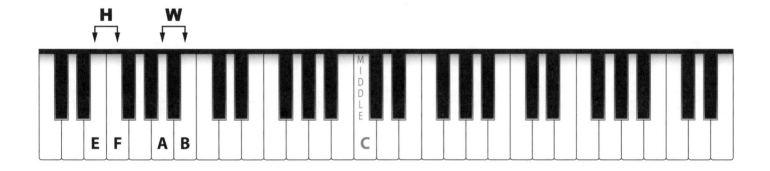

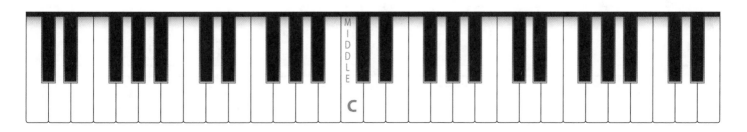

Intervals - 2nds

On the piano's keyboard, the interval from one white key to the next adjacent white key is a 2nd. When played in a row they are considered melodic 2nd intervals. If played together they would be harmonic 2nd intervals. A 2nd in music notation will be from line to the next space; or, space to the next line. As you progress you must train your ear to hear different intervals so you can learn and write your own music effectively. Play the following 2nd intervals and make sure to hear their unique sound.

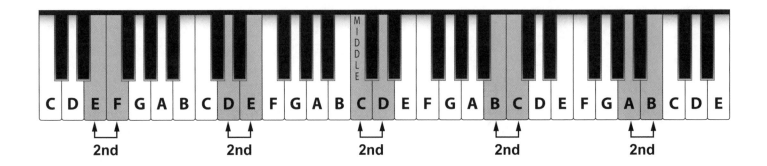

2nds Etude

Here is an etude that has many 2nd intervals included. See if you can locate all the 2nds within this piece. The coordination between both hands may be difficult in the beginning. Try each hand separately first, then put them both together.

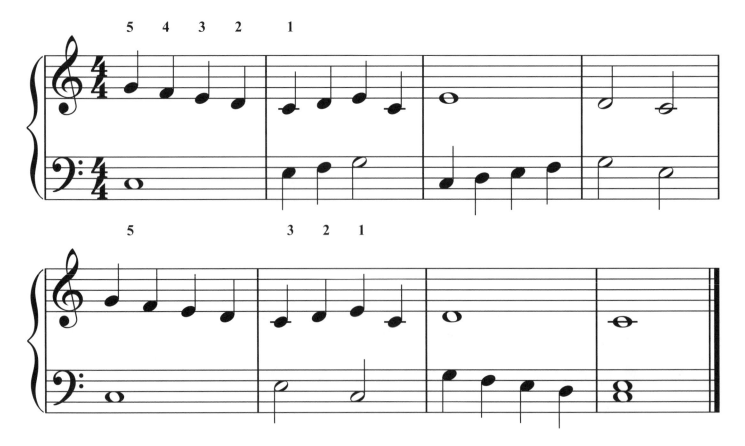

72

Intervals - 3rds

On the keyboard a 3rd interval is two white keys away from any white key. A 3rd interval in music notation is from any line or space to the next. If there are three keys up to the second note it will be a minor 3rd, if there are four keys it is a major 3rd. Play the notes in a row and you can hear that the major 3rd sounds happy while the minor 3rd sounds sad. Again make sure to listen to the 3rd interval and hear its unique sound. Play the examples below:

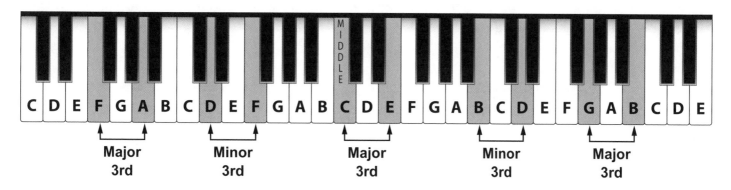

3rds Etude

Here is an etude that has many 3rd intervals included. See if you can locate all the 3rds within this piece.

Andante

Seeing Intervals

An important thing to note: in music notation all even numbered intervals, such as 2nds or 4ths will always go from a line to space or space to line. In turn, all odd number intervals like 3rds or 5ths will always go from line to line or space to space. If the intervals are played in a row they are called melodic intervals, if played together they are called harmonic intervals. Play the 2nd and 3rd intervals below and connect the way they look with their sound.

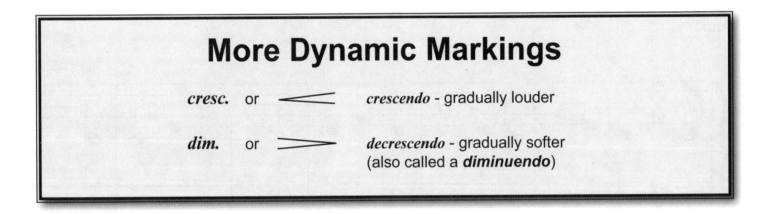

Alternate Fingerings

In the next two songs there will be alternate fingerings that you will use. I have depicted these fingerings with circles around them. In Brahms' "Lullaby" you will be extending the notes higher with your right hand. In "This Land is Your Land" you will extend the right hand lower using a cross over. Pay attention to these fingering to play these songs properly. You will be expanding your reach on the keyboard more and more as you progress.

Brahms' Lullaby

This Land is Your Land

Allegro

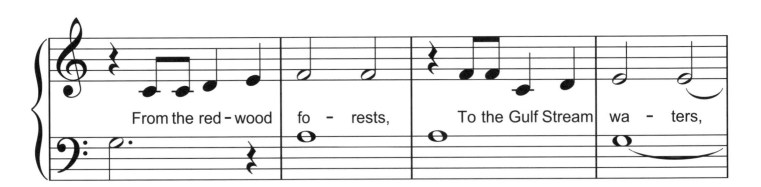

Crossover

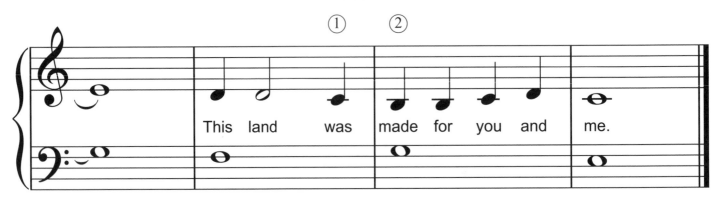

Intervals - 4ths & 5ths

Fourths

To play a 4th you skip two white keys.

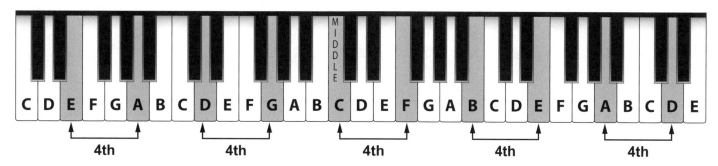

Fifths

To play a 5th you skip 3 white keys.

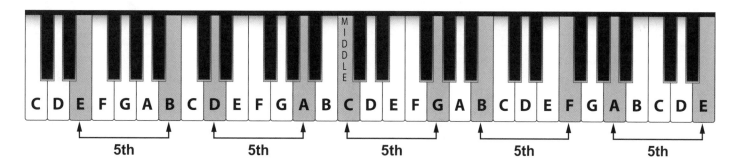

An important thing to remember, 4ths will always go from a line to space or space to line and 5ths will always go from line to line or space to space. Play the 4th and 5th intervals below and train your ears to hear their sound.

4ths Etude

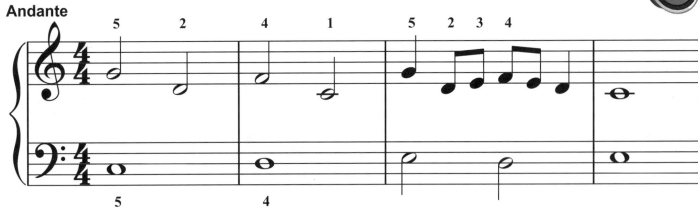

5ths Etude

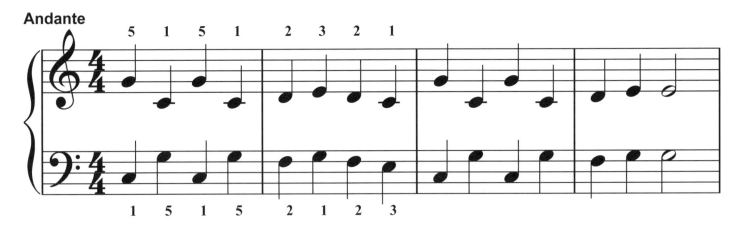

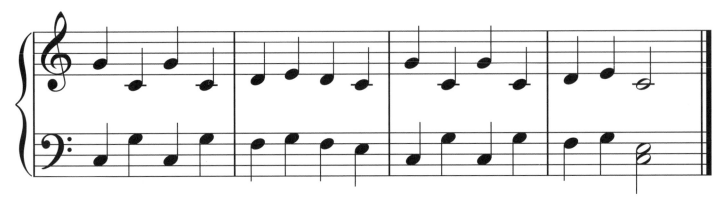

Oh! Susanna

In this song there is a C major chord played with the left hand. Notice how the C major chord is a 3rd and 5th interval together. Intervals are combined to create chords.

Allegro

79

America (My Country Tis of Thee)

In this song you will find 2nd, 3rd and 5th intervals. Many times the left and right hand noted together form chords.

Andante

Kum-Ba-Ya

The Major Scale Formula

The major scale is the mother of all music. I call it this because most music starts from the major scale. There is a formula used to create a major scale using a series of whole steps and half steps. The pattern is: whole step, whole step, half step, whole step, whole step, whole step, half step, or commonly written:

W – W – H – W – W – W – H

If you start on any note and use this formula you will create a major scale. The starting note will also be the root note (or key). Here's an example: start with a root note middle C and play the C major scale.

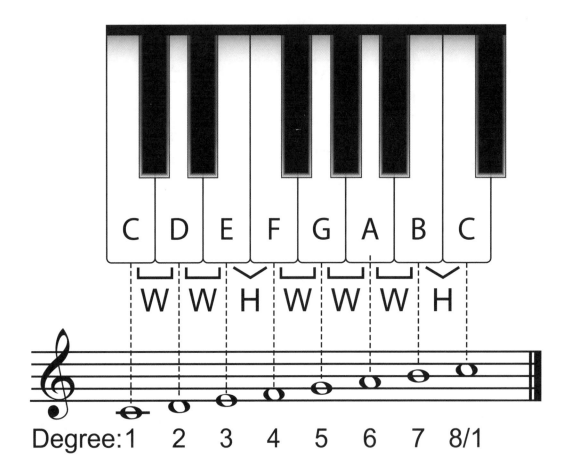

The C major scale is C – D – E – F – G – A – B – C. This will be the only natural scale, meaning the only major scale that won't need any sharps or flats to make the formula work. Every other scale will have at least one flat or one sharp.

Playing the C Major Scale

Because there are eight notes in the major scale to play this scale with one hand you will need to learn two finger crossings. For both of these crossings it is VERY important not to twist your wrist and to keep your fingers curved and palm open.

Ascending Cross Under

To play the C major scale ascending, start with your right hand thumb on the middle C and play C – D – E. Next cross your thumb under your middle finger to play the F note, and then continue with G – A – B – C. Follow the diagram below to play the C major scale ascending.

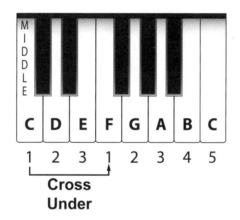

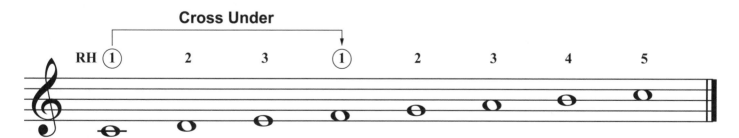

Descending Cross Over

Start at the last note of the scale with your pinky on the C note. Play down the scale C – B – A – G – F, then cross your middle finger over your thumb to the E note and finish the scale. Follow the diagram below to play the C major scale descending.

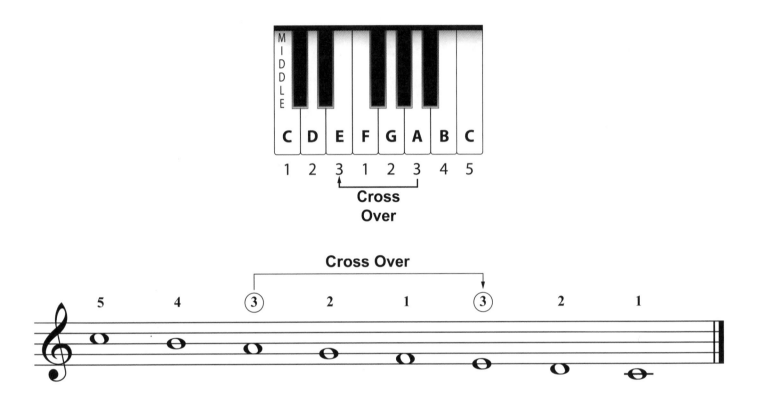

C Major Scale Left Hand

To play the C major scale with your left hand you will also have two finger crossings but they will be the opposite of the right hand. You will cross over ascending and under descending. To the right is a picture of the finger crossing with your left hand. Play the left hand C major scale on the next page.

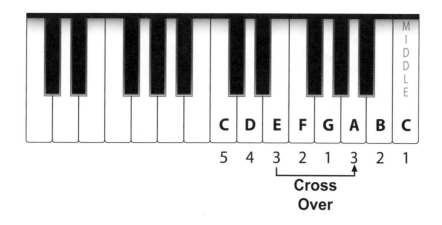

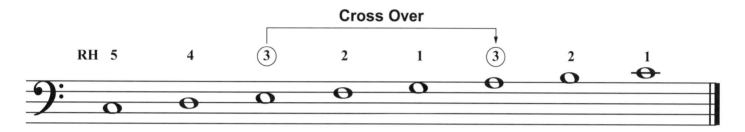

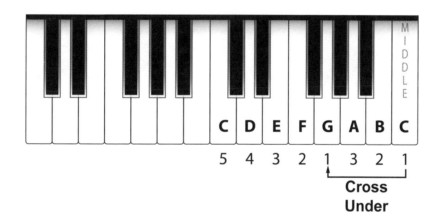

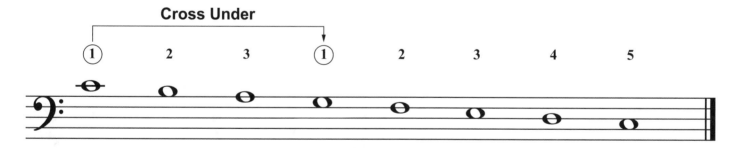

Learn Piano 2 - Quiz 2

Once you complete this section go to RockHouseMethod.com and take the quiz to track your progress. You will receive an email with your results and suggestions.

G Major Chord

Let's learn a new major chord. You will use the 4 – 3 method to find the notes to play the G major chord. Follow the diagram below and make sure to use the proper fingers:

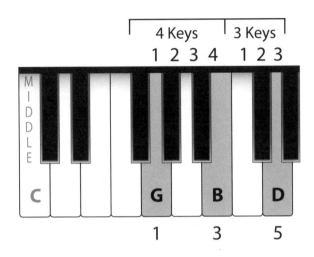

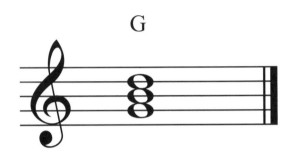

The I – IV – V Chords

The I – IV – V chords are the most common chord combination in all music. Many hit songs have been written using this song structure. It is called a I – IV – V progression because you build chords from the 1st, 4th and 5th notes in the major scale. A I – IV – V progression in the key of "C" would be C – F and G major chords. Below are the diagrams for all three chords. Play them one after another and hear the sound of this chord progression.

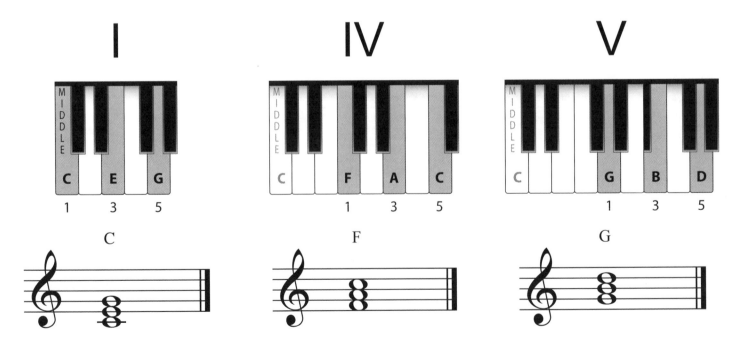

Adding Bass Notes

Now add a lower note to each chord as a bass note. This gives the chord a full sound almost like adding a bass guitar. Play each of the I – IV – V chords with the bass notes.

C Major

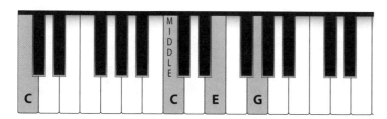

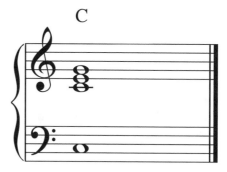

F Major

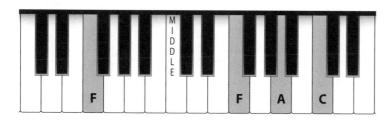

G Major

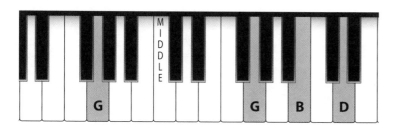

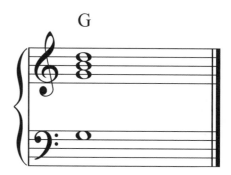

The I – IV – V 12 Bar Blues

The I – IV – V progression is often used in a 12 bar blues structure. This means that there are 12 measures that form the progression before repeating. Below is a 12 bar blues progression:

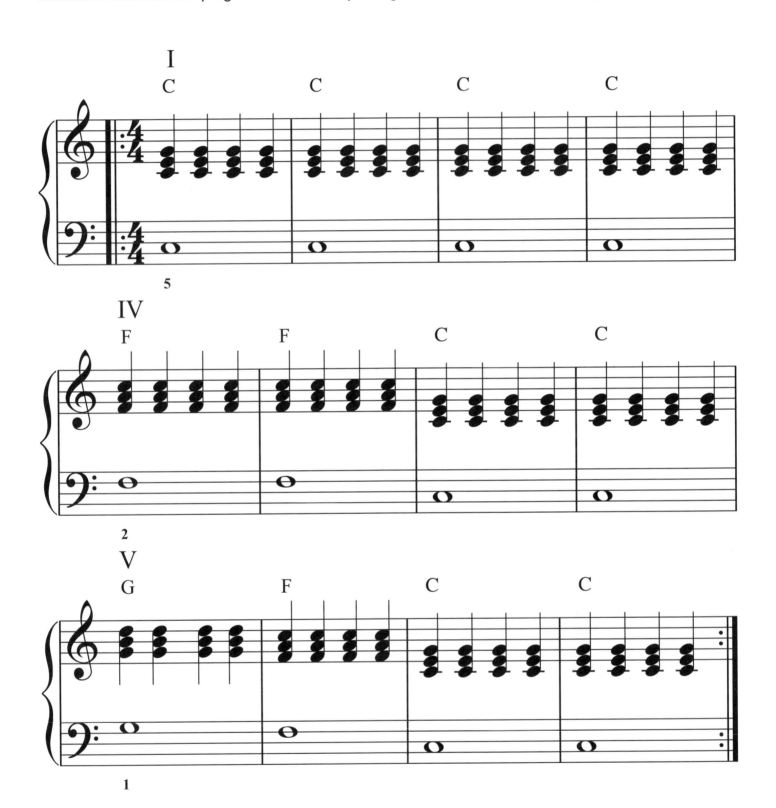

Chord Inversions

An inversion, by definition, is to turn something upside down. For chord inversions you take the notes and rearrange them in a different order. One reason this is done is to keep your hand in a small area on the keyboard and still be able to play many chords. We will be constructing 1st inversions for the C, F and G major chords. To play a 1st inversion take the bottom note (root note) and move it to the top of the chord. For the C major chord take the C note and move it to the top and the chord notes will be E – G – C. See the diagram below and play this inversion:

C Major

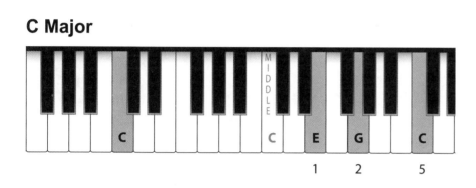

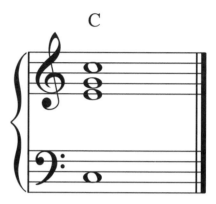

C

Next, play the 1st inversion F and G major chords in the same fashion. For F major, take the F note and move it to the top so the order would be A – C – F. For G major take the G root note and move it to the top of the chord so the notes in order will be B – D – G. I have presented these two chords an octave lower then you played them previously because you will use them this way in the next lesson. After you play the chord with the right hand add the left hand bass note.

F Major

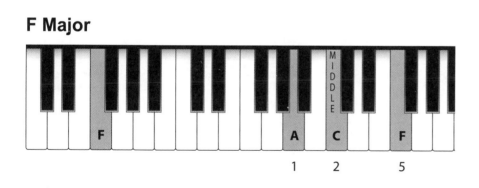

F

G Major

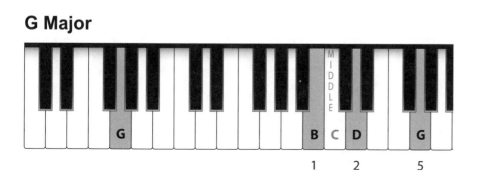

G

The Blues Feel

The 12 bar blues you learned had a steady quarter note feel. The blues often has uneven or syncopated rhythms. One common blues feel combines eighth, dotted quarter and quarter notes to create a syncopated rhythm. Play the following rhythm example to understand the feel. The last chord is played with staccato and should be cut short.

The Blues Shuffle

Next, you will apply this blues feel to the 12 bar blues using the chord inversions for the F and G chords; make sure to play over the backing track to apply this lesson in a band fashion. The last measure contains eighth notes that should be played with a blues swing feel to them and not played as even eighth notes.

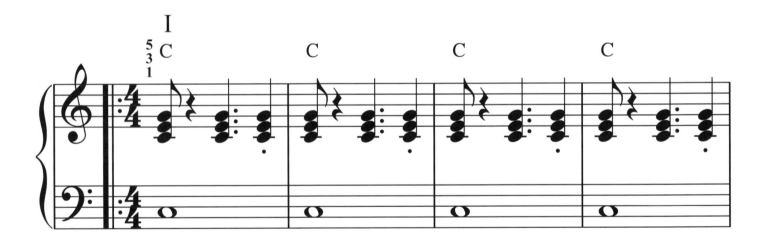

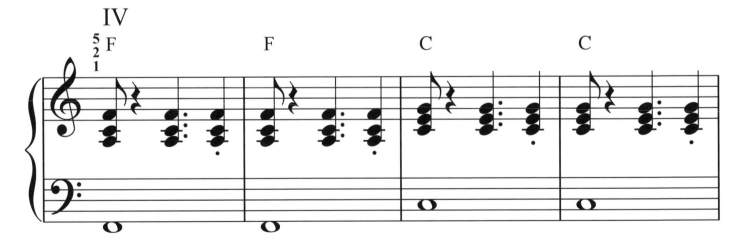

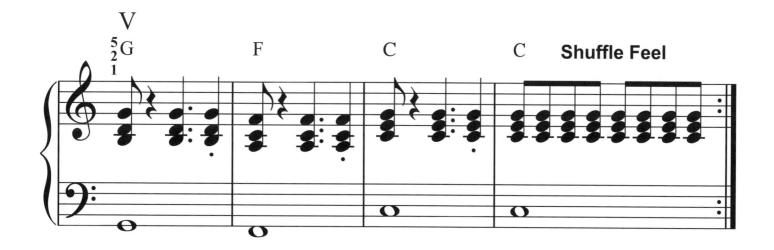

Canon

Canon is a very popular classical progression. I have outlined the chord progression above the staff so you can see and hear where each chord is played. You will be playing intervals that you learned earlier in the book with your right hand, take note of these. The intervals played with G and F are inverted 5ths. This means that the root is on top and the interval becomes a 4th stacked this way. We will get deeper into theory of intervals in Book 3.

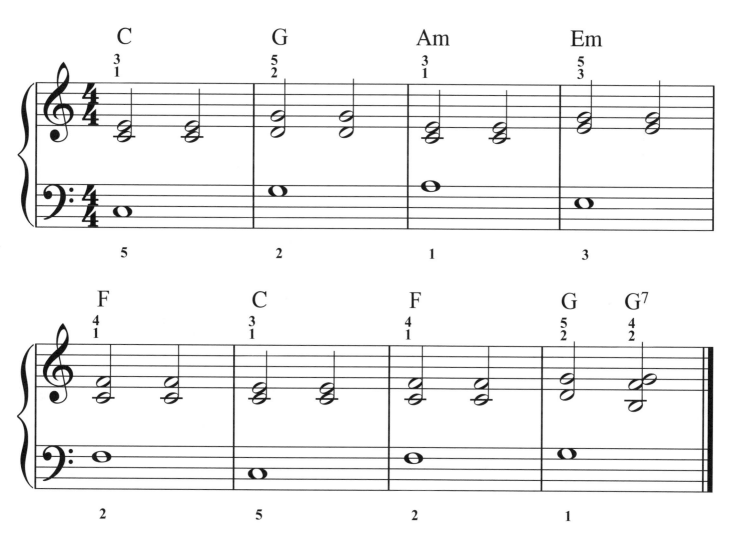

First & Second Endings

Sometimes a composer wants to repeat a section in a song and add a different ending but doesn't want to write out everything all over again creating pages and pages of music. This is where first and second endings come in. First and second endings are notated by numbered brackets over each ending. The endings can be any number of measures in length. In the example below each ending is one measure in length. Note the repeat sign between the endings. This means that you play through ending one, go back to the beginning play up to the first ending, skip the first ending and play the second ending. Play through the example below. In the next lesson you will use first and second endings within a song.

Dreaming Messiah

Primary Chords

Chords derived from the root, 4th and 5th degrees of a major scale are called primary chords. You have already learned to play the I – IV – V chords in the key of "C" major, now you will learn where they come from. On the staff below, if you only played the bottom note of each chord you would play a C major scale. Notice all of the chords, as well as the primary chords, are derived from the C major scale.

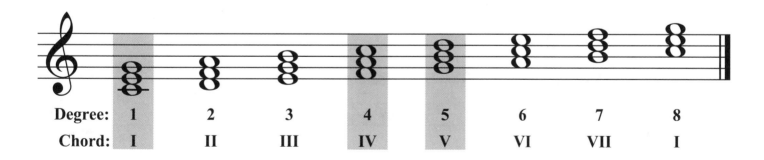

Sixteenth Notes

To play the following exercises you will need to know sixteenth notes. A sixteenth note receives ¼ beat of sound. It subdivides one beat into four equal sections. Sixteenth notes are twice as fast as an eighth note. Count sixteenth notes now as follows:

Now play sixteenth notes with the C major chord to understand and feel the timing. Accent the first note of each four note sequence to accentuate the feel of this timing.

Single Note Exercises #2

Here are more exercises to help challenge your hands to build coordination. Make sure to keep the notes in a steady tempo and build up speed gradually. I recommend using a metronome to help gauge your progress. Write down your metronome tempos and see how much speed you can develop in a few weeks time. These exercises should be practiced daily. Even experienced players still practice these to warm their fingers up before playing.

Example 1 - Right Hand

Example 2 - Right Hand

Example 3 - Left Hand

Example 4 - Left Hand

The Star Spangled Banner

This song introduces a lower A note being played with your right hand. Look at the keyboard diagram to see the notes location.

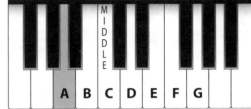

Andante

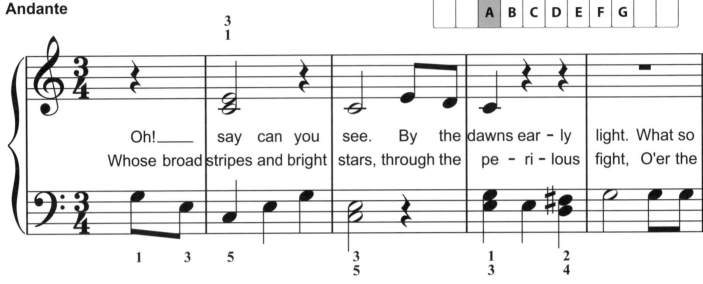

Oh!___ say can you see. By the dawns ear - ly light. What so
Whose broad stripes and bright stars, through the pe - ri - lous fight, O'er the

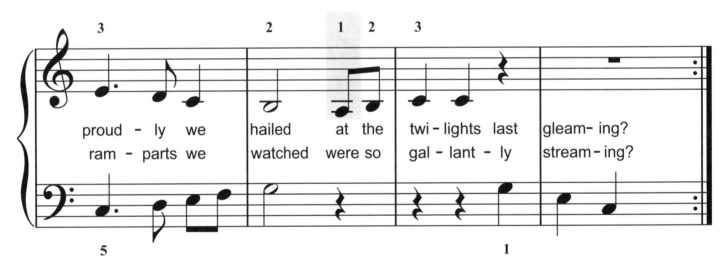

proud - ly we hailed at the twi - lights last gleam- ing?
ram - parts we watched were so gal - lant - ly stream- ing?

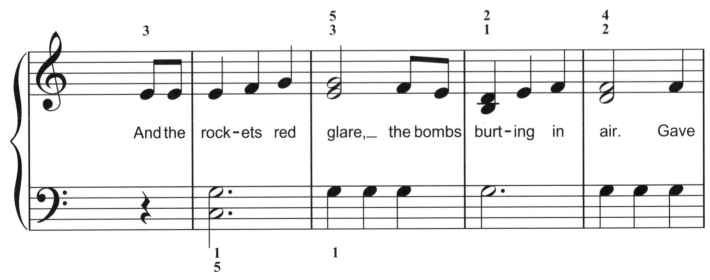

And the rock-ets red glare,_ the bombs burt-ing in air. Gave

proof   to   the   night   that   our   flag   was   still   there.   -   Oh

say   does   that___   Star-Span-gled   Ban-ner___   yet___   wave___   O'er the

Slower

rit.

land_____ of the   free   and the   home   of   the   brave!

Fermata

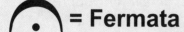 **= Fermata**

A fermata indicates that a note is sustained longer than its written note value. The exact time of how long its held is at the discretion of the performer; however, a sustained note that is double the time value is not unusual. I have outlined in the previous song where you will find the fermata.

Spring

From *The Four Seasons*

A. Vivaldi

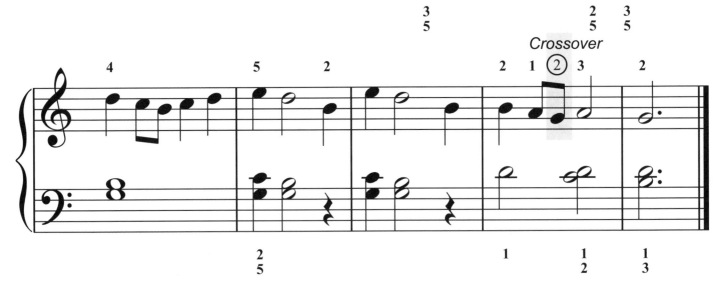

Learn Piano 2 - Quiz 3

Congratulations you've made it to the end of Book 2! Go to RockHouseMethod.com and take the quiz to track your progress. You will receive an email with your results and an official Rock House Method "Certificate of Completion" when you pass.

Book 3 Table of Contents

Words from the Author

To learn a new language you take small steps, progressively increasing your knowledge until you speak it fluidly. Music is the language you are learning. With consistent practice this book will take you to the next level, attaining your goal to play music. In this book you will learn the important basics to build a solid foundation of music. Don't just play; take time to listen to what you are playing as well as other musicians. When your ears hear and understand music, your fingers will respond. So lets get to our pianos, open our ears and mind and let's play music.

Key of G Major

In the key signature you see what notes will be sharped or flatted within a song. In order for a song to stay within a major key it has to follow the major scale formula you learned earlier. In the key of G major there is one sharped needed F# to keep the order of whole and half steps correct. See how this is noted below.

W W H W W W H
G – A – B – C – D – E – F# – G

The G Major Scale

Before you learn songs in the key of G you need to learn to play the G major scale. You will use the same cross over and cross under fingering as you learned with the C major scale.

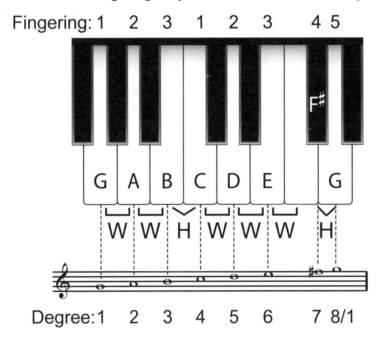

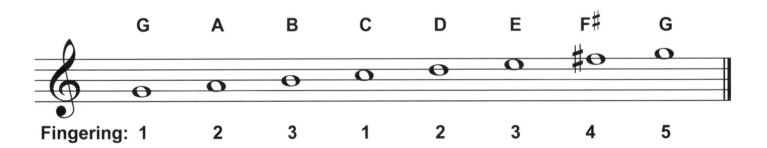

Key Signature of G Major

The key signature indicates notes that will be altered within a song. In the key of G you learned that all the F notes will be F#. Instead of placing sharp signs before every F note you can put an F# at the beginning of every staff. This will tell players that this song is in the key of G and that every F will be sharped unless indicated by a natural sign. To the right is what the key signature of G will look like.

Articulations

In music notation there are several symbols that will tell you how to play the notes. Below are some of the most common you will see. You have learned a few of these in book 2 but take time to review them, you will be playing them in the coming songs.

Phrasing Slur

This curved line that connects a group of notes indicates that you play them smoothly together in a flowing motion.

Accent

An accent is a small arrow placed on top or bottom of a note that indicates that you play the note louder.

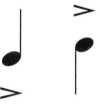

Staccato

A staccato articulation is a small dot placed on top or bottom of a note that indicates that you cut the note short and detached not letting it ring out.

Natural Sign

In the key of G major you will play all the F notes as F# unless indicated by a natural sign. In the next song you will be playing in the key of G major.

Home On the Range

Minuet in G

J.S. Bach

Greensleeves

This song is written in 3/4 timing. Pay attention to the first and second endings that occur twice within this song.

Moderato

Here Comes the Bride

Canon

Andante

The Key of F Major

Another common key is F major. The key signature of F major will have one flat, the Bb. The reason it has one flat is to make the order of half and whole steps work starting from the F note.

$$W \quad W \quad H \quad W \quad W \quad W \quad H$$
$$F - G - A - B^{\flat} - C - D - E - F$$

The F Major Scale

Before you learn any songs in the key of F major you need to learn how to play the F major scale. Notice the fingering is different in the left hand because the Bb note falls on a black key. You thumb has to cross under after the 4th finger which is a little bit more of a stretch then before.

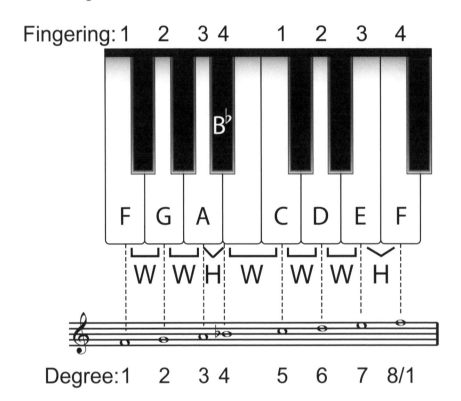

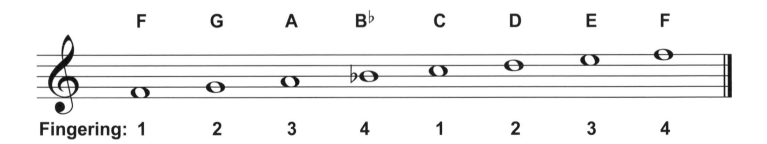

Key Signature of F Major

The F major key signature indicates notes that in the key of F you just learned all of the B notes will be B♭. Instead of placing flat (♭) signs before every B note you can put an B♭ at the beginning of every staff. This will tell players that this song is in the key of F and that every B will be flatted unless indicated by a natural sign. To the right is what the key signature of F major will look like.

Triplets

Eighth and sixteenth notes subdivide a beat in half and quarters. These are even number breakdowns of 2 and 4. Triplets subdivide a beat into threes. For every one beat, you're going to play three notes. Count triplets like this:

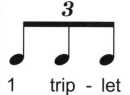

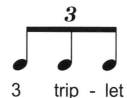
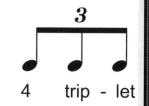

Now play triplets using the notes of the C major chord to understand and feel triplet timing.

Accent the down beat that falls on each number to accentuate the triplet feel. The accent is represented by the ">" symbol above the note. Triplets can be found in every genre of music.

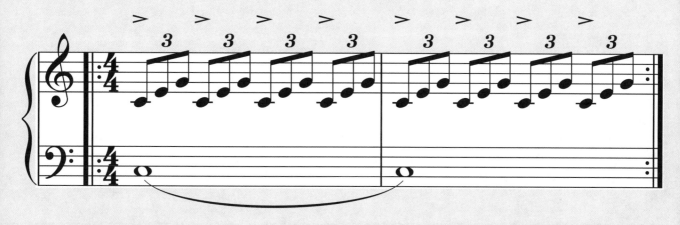

Jesus, Joy of Man's Desiring

Here is a great Bach piece that incorporates triplet timing. This piece is in the key of "F" major so make sure to flat the B notes. The left hand is playing quarter notes against the right hand triplets.

Andante

Learn Piano 3 - Quiz 1
Once you complete this section go to RockHouseMethod.com and take the quiz to track your progress. You will receive an email with your results and suggestions.

Ol' Smokey

Moderato

111

Minor Chords

Minor chords have a sad sound compared to the bright happy sound of major chords you previously learned. Minor chords are often written with a capital letter followed by a lower case m. There is an easy method for forming minor chords which I call the 3 – 4 method. By counting up three keys (half steps) then four keys (half steps) from any note you form a minor chord. Let's form a D minor chord. Start with the D note, count up three keys this is the F note. Next count up four keys, this is the A note. The D minor chord contains the notes D – F – A played together.

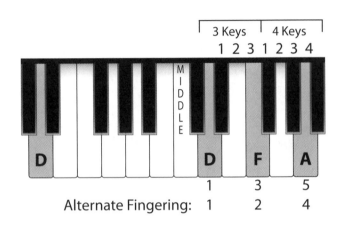

Dm

Let's learn the E and A minor chords next.

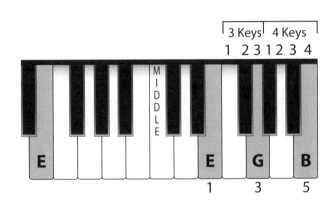

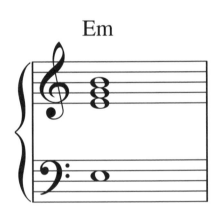

Em

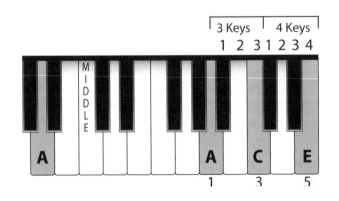

Am

2nd Inversions

As you learned to make a 1st inversion of a chord you take the root or bottom note and move it up an octave higher. For 2nd inversions you take the bottom two notes and move them up one octave. Below are 2nd inversions for the G major and A minor chords.

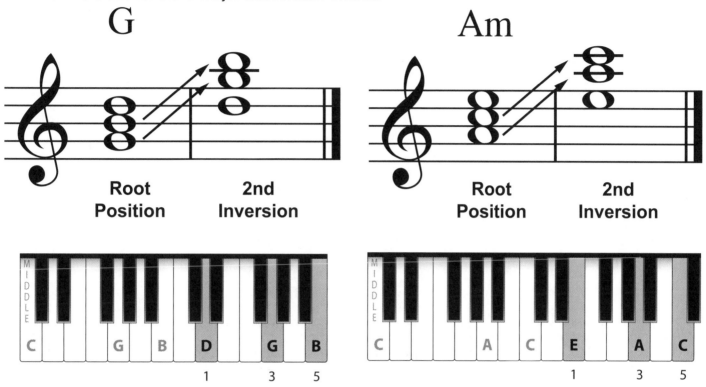

Minor Chord Progression

Let's put these minor chords into action and play a minor chord progression. This progression will go as follows Am – Em – Dm – G. I have given two variations one in a half note timing playing each chord two times per measure, the second in quarter note timing where you will play each chord four times per measure. Once you get the changes under your fingers add the bass root note with your left hand. You can play this along with the backing track; this will help you get comfortable playing with other musicians.

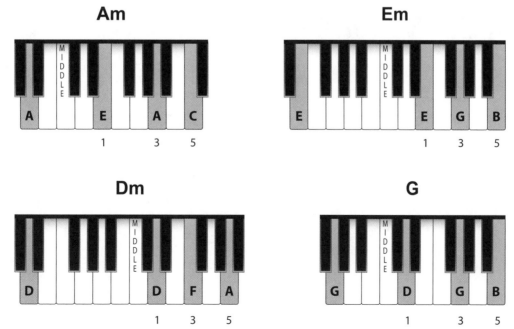

Example 1

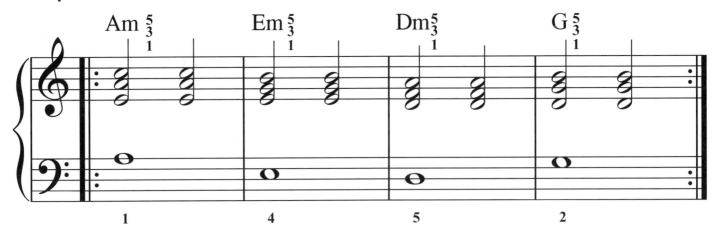

Example 2

In this example your right hand plays quarter notes. The left hand plays half notes with A, E and G one octave lower.

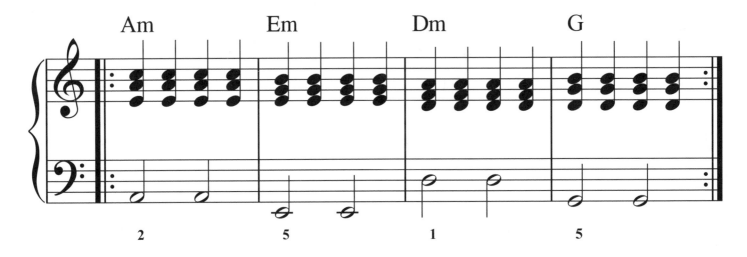

Rocking the Minor Chords

Here is a variation of the rhythm from the last lesson. The pattern here is to play the top two notes of the chord then the bottom note only, back and forth. This rocking motion creates a great movement in the rhythm giving it a new sound. Make sure to keep the left hand bass root notes for each chord. Play this rhythm over the same backing track and see how this variation changes the feel of the song.

More Major Chords

The A and E major chords are similar. Your 3rd finger will be playing a back key in the middle on both. Your hand position will stay the same on each. The more chords you are familiar with the easier it will be for you to learn songs.

A Major

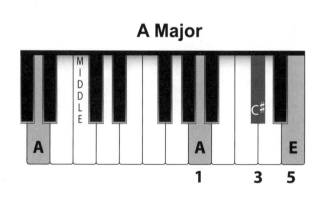

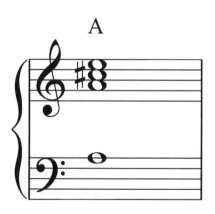

E Major

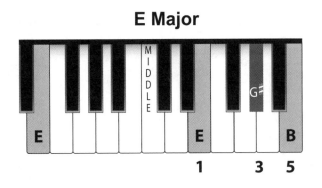

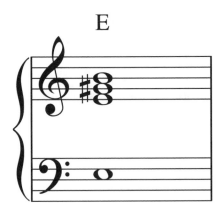

Major Chord Inversions

Now let's make 1st inversions for the A and G major chords. As you learned just take the root note and bring it up one octave. These two inversions will be used in the following lesson.

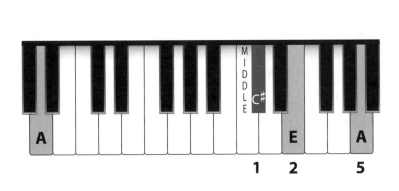

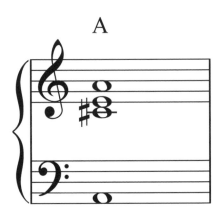

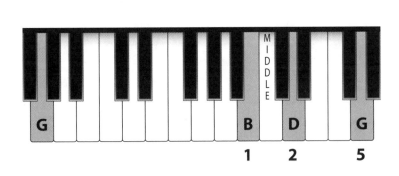

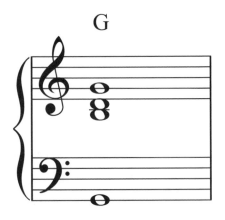

Major Song Progression

Before you play the progression play each of the four chords in succession. Notice how with the inversions included the chord changes are very easy to make. Next play the song first with steady quarter notes then add the rocking variation you learned previously.

House of the Rising Sun

This song has left hand chords that play the complete rhythm to the song while the right hand plays the melody. Play the rhythm chords first; this will help you to hear the structure of the song. Next play the melody by it self before putting both parts together. Play the song with the backing track and get familiar playing with other musicians.

Moderato

Chord Review

For this chord review you will use all the major and minor chords you have learned so far. Play each with your left hand starting with the lowest possible notes and then play that same chord one octave up with your right hand and keep playing the chord up one octave switching hands all the way across the keyboard. Follow the diagrams below.

G Major

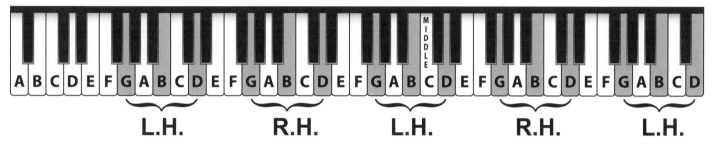

F Major

E Minor

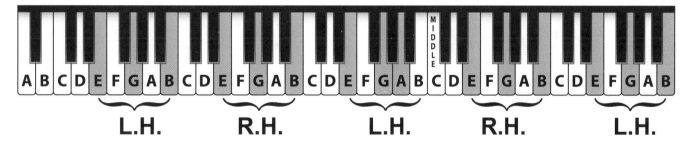

A Minor

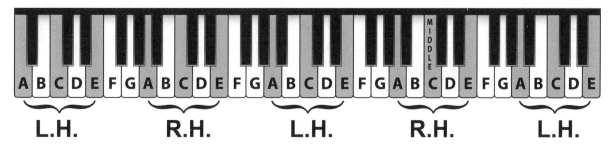

Take Me Out To the Ball Game

Moderato

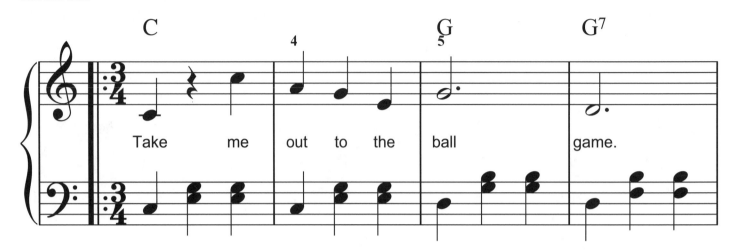

Take me out to the ball game.

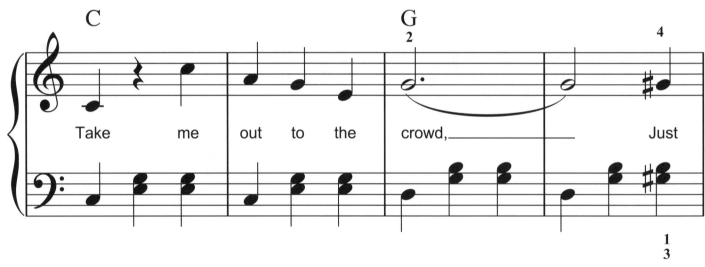

Take me out to the crowd,_____ Just

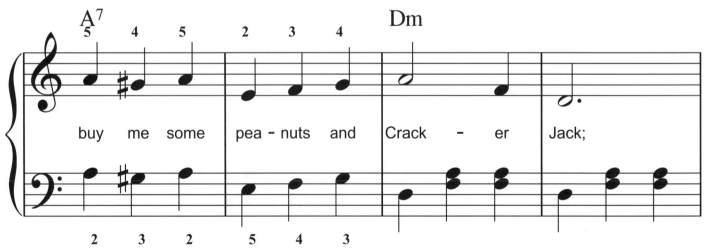

buy me some pea - nuts and Crack - er Jack;

Learn Piano 3 - Quiz 2
Once you complete this section go to RockHouseMethod.com/quiz and take the quiz to track your progress. You will receive an email with your results and suggestions.

Single Note Exercise #3

In this chapter you will play a series of challenging finger exercises. Make sure to start each slowly and build up speed gradually. I recommend that you use a metronome while practicing these exercises. Start at a speed that you can play the exercise completely without making any mistakes; then, increase your speed in small increments. Write the tempo you attain each day on a separate piece of paper or inside your book to track your progress.

Right Hand - Ascending

Right Hand - Descending

Left Hand - Ascending

Left Hand - Descending

Toccata in D Minor

The Blues

The blues has influenced just about every genre of music. Having a good understanding of the blues will make you a better player. The blues is often known as a feel and emotion that makes your body sway along. In this chapter you will learn the basics that will help you play the blues.

Left Hand Blues

Here is a C blues rhythm that you will play with your left hand. You will be hitting two notes together going through three chord variations in a 12 bar blues format. Start with C and G, then C and A hitting each two times repetitively. This is a difficult rhythm to play so take your time. Once you feel comfortable with the changes play this with the backing track

The Shuffle Feel

The shuffle feel is an uneven rhythm also known as the swing feel. This rhythm is used by many blues greats. In the example on the next page see how this feel is created by taking out the middle note of a triplet. Play the rhythm from the last lesson with the shuffle feel. I've outlined the first section below. Once you can play the feel apply it to the complete rhythm from the previous lesson

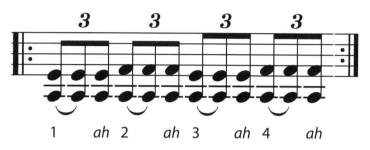

Shuffle Feel Symbol

You will find that composers use a symbol above a staff to denote that there will be a shuffle feel. Here is what this will look like. You see a triplet "equals" two eighth notes. When you see this on a piece of music, make sure to play with a shuffle feel.

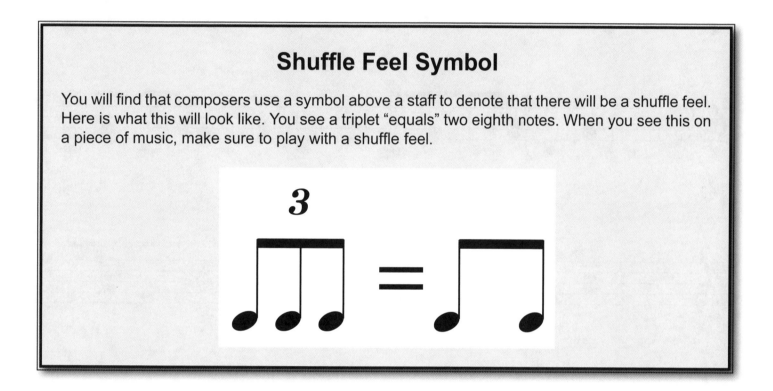

Right Hand Blues Rhythm

The right hand often plays rhythm patterns in blues music. This rhythm pattern pivots off the middle C note. The coordination of playing fingers 2 & 4 and 3 & 5 is a bit challenging. This rhythm will be used in the next song so make sure to have it mastered before moving on.

Right Hand Blues

This blues rhythm is eighth notes with an eighth note rest starting each measure. This creates an up beat syncopation that gives it a great blues sound. Play through it slowly and build speed up gradually. Once you feel comfortable playing the entire progression play it over the backing track.

Dominant Seventh Chords

Dominant seventh chords are 4-note chords that are commonly used in blues progressions. They have a "funky" or "bluesy" quality to them which give music a feeling of movement.

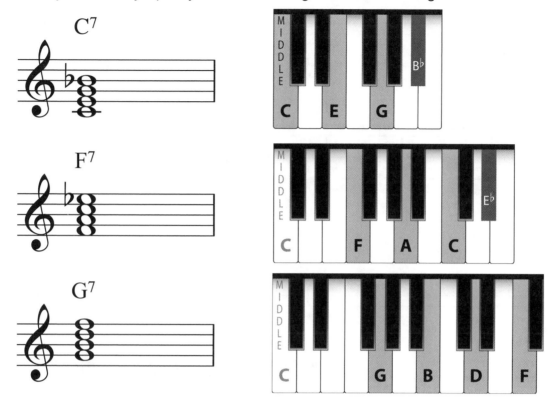

Dominant Seventh Chord Voicings

A full dominant seventh chord has four notes but many times there are inversions used that omit the 5th degree. These voicings are still considered dominant seventh chords. Here are a few that are common for you to play.

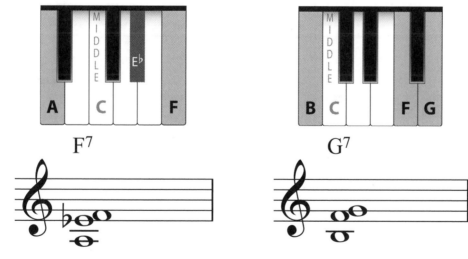

Left Hand Bass Lines

Many times your left hand will play bass lines similar to what a bass player would play. Here are two examples to challenge your fingers. I have added the dominant seventh chords for the right hand to play along with each. Add these chords after you can play the bass lines completely from start to finish. Once you can play both hands together play each example over the backing track.

Example 1

Example 2

Left Hand Chord Rhythms

Often times your left hand will play chords while the right hand plays a melody. In this fashion you are essentially play rhythm and melody at the same time. Although you have played a few songs that contained left hand chords the following song Joy to the World contains a more structured chord rhythm. You have learned that the primary chords in a key are the I – IV – V in book 2. For the key of F major the I – IV – V chords are F major, Bb major and C dominant 7th. These three chords are found in the rhythm to this song, below I've outlined some of the inversions.

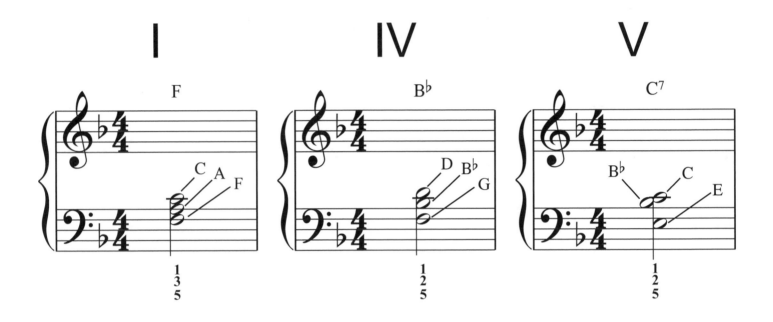

Joy to the World

Moderato

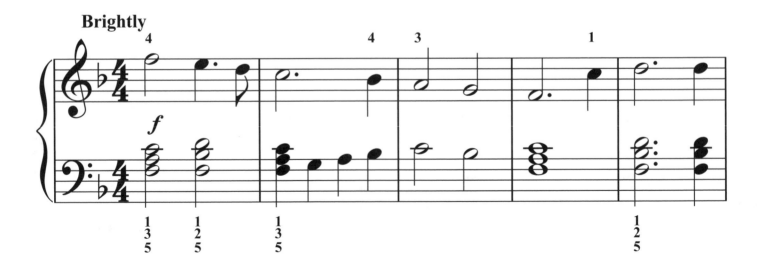

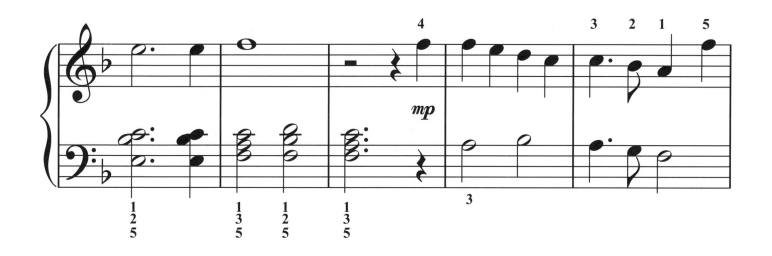

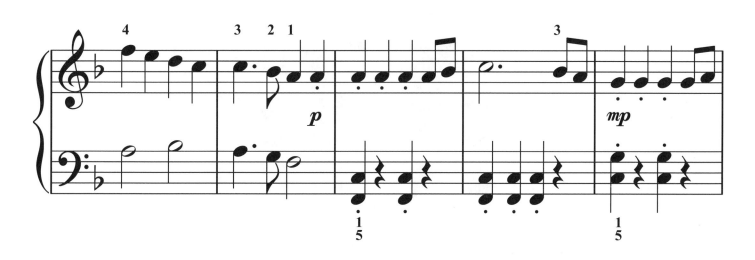

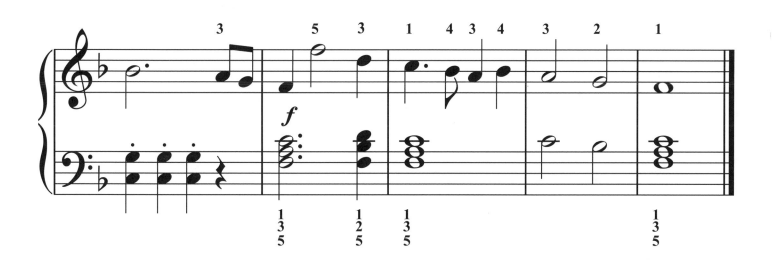

Minor Pentatonic Scale Key of "C"

Minor Pentatonic scales are the most widely used scales in rock and blues music. This is a five note scale, which means that it repeats after five scale degrees back in a circle type fashion. The notes included in the C minor pentatonic scale are C – Eb – F – G – Bb.

Scales are your alphabet for creating leads and melodies. Just like you learned your alphabet in school and then expanded into words, sentences and complete stories you will learn scales for piano then expand to melodies, leads and complete songs. Play the C minor pentatonic scale below and get familiar with its distinct sound.

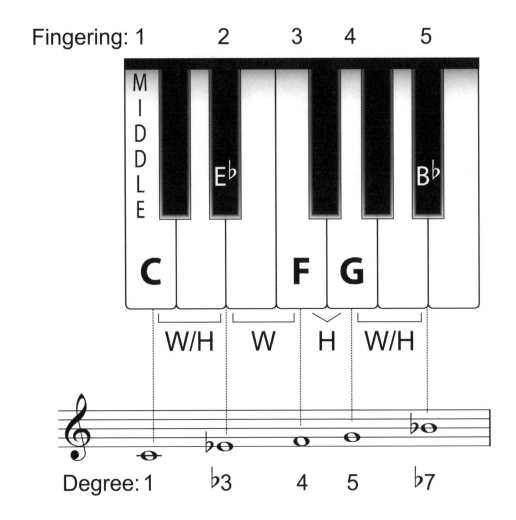

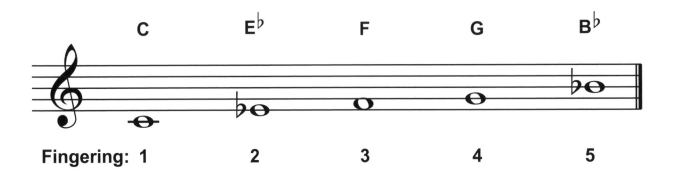

Blues Phrases

Now it's time to have a little fun. This group of five notes can be easily used to create blues sounding melodies. By mixing these notes up into little phrases or groups of notes you can create your own melodies. I have given you a few examples to start you off. Play these then create your own. Be sure to play them over the backing track.

Example 1

Example 2

Example 3

Single Note Exercise #4

Right Hand - Ascending

Right Hand - Descending

Left Hand - Ascending

Carol of the Bells

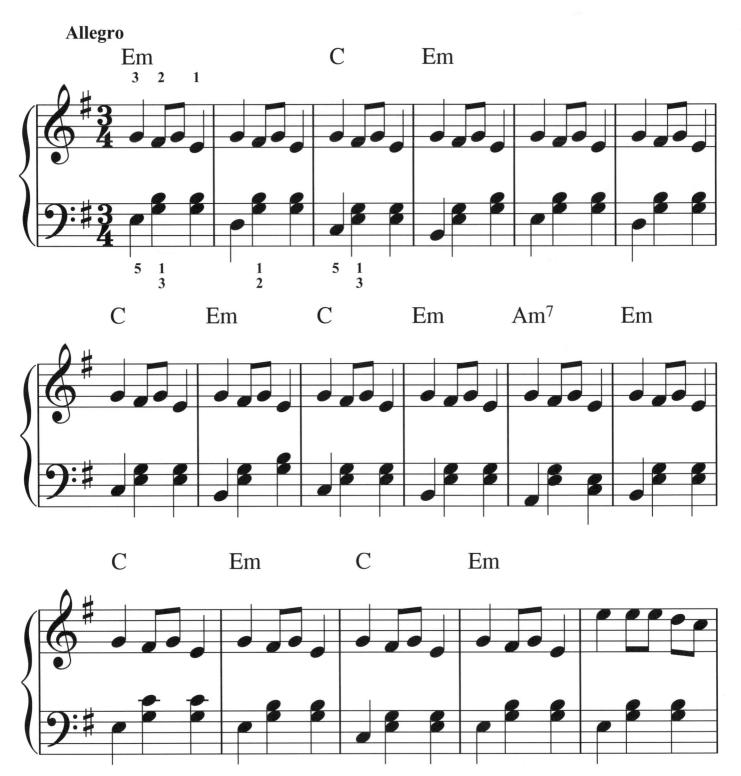

The Entertainer

Allegro

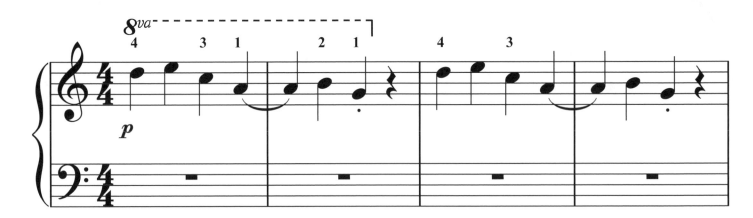

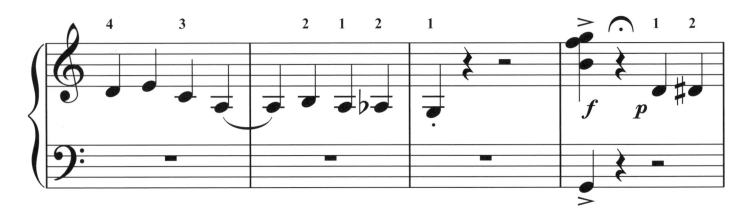

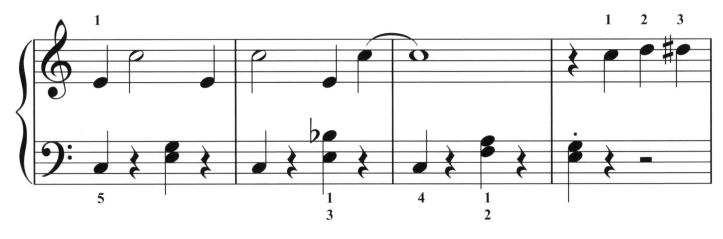

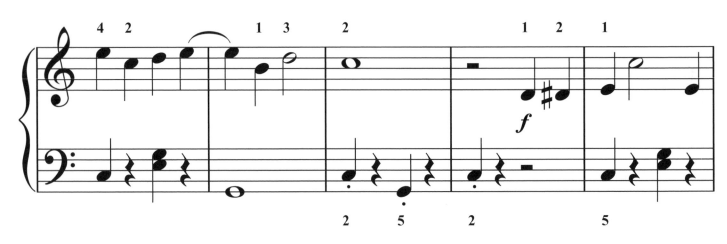

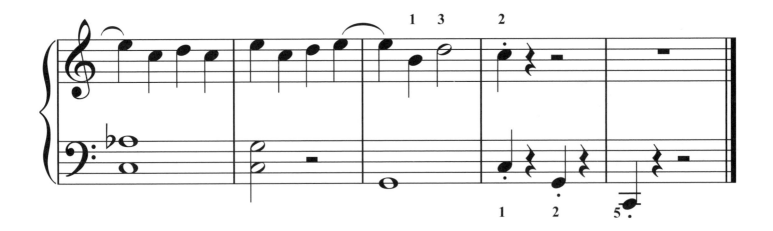

Left Hand Finger Patterns

Many songs will include left hand finger patterns. The first four measure of the following Piano Sonata in C Major include this type of a finger pattern. These patterns can be challenging to play. When there is a challenging section in a song you should isolate the section and play it repetitively before playing the complete piece. Below is an exercise to practice that will prepare you to play the finger pattern in the next song.

Piano Sonata in C Major

W.A. Mozart

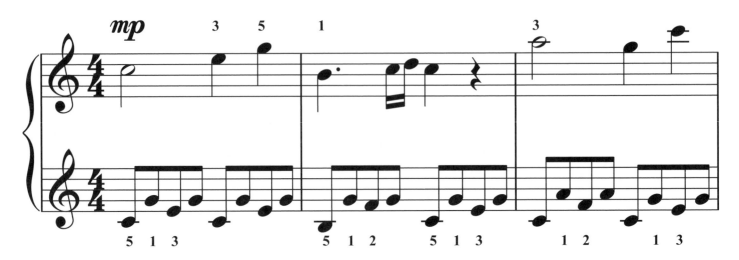

143

Learn Piano 3 - Quiz 3
Congratulations you've made it to the end of Book 3! Go to RockHouseMethod.com and take the quiz to track your progress. You will receive an email with your results and an official Rock House Method "Certificate of Completion" when you pass.

KEY TAB

Exclusive Key Tablature For Accelerated Learning

How To Read Key Tab

Key Tab is a system for reading music on the piano or keyboard that was created by John McCarthy as a Rock House exclusive. This system helps piano players learn chord progressions and songs quickly and easily.

The Key Tab staff is divided in two an upper and lower half by the count of the timing. The upper section is designed for notes played with your right and while the lower section is for notes played with the left hand. The letters placed on the staff lines designate the name of the note to play. There is an octave range indicator at the beginning of the staff for both left and right hands, this will tell you which octave the notes are played in from C notes. The "0" octave is from middle C "+1" would be one octave up and "-1" would be one octave lower. There is a number placed before the note names which indicates the finger used to play the note.

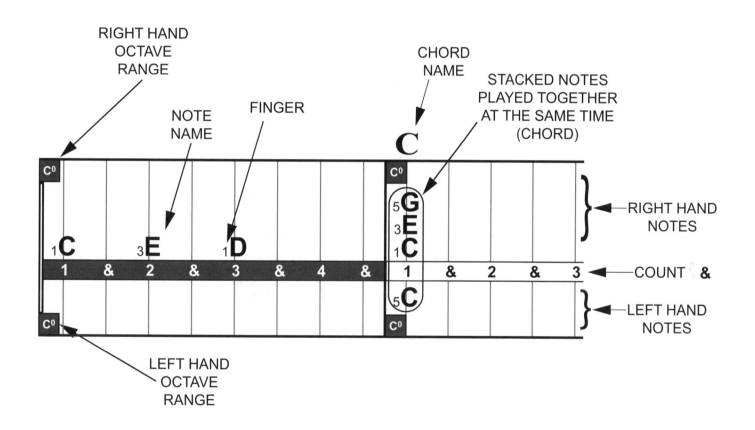

Study the diagram above to understand how Key Tab works an before you move on to this section of the book.

Chords

Below are chords that you will use to play songs using Key Tab. Memorize the fingerings and practice these chords across your keyboard.

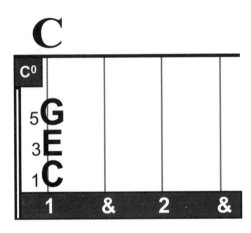

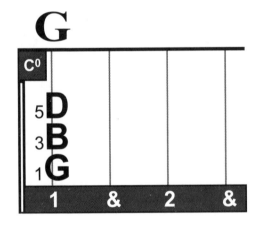

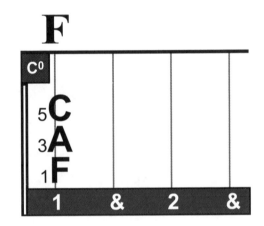

The 1- 4 Progression

The following chord progression is a very popular yet simple progression. It is called a 1 – 4 progression because F is four scale degrees above the root chord C. The chords are played in a quester note rhythm so you will sound the chord on each count.

C – D – E – F
1 – 2 – 3 – 4

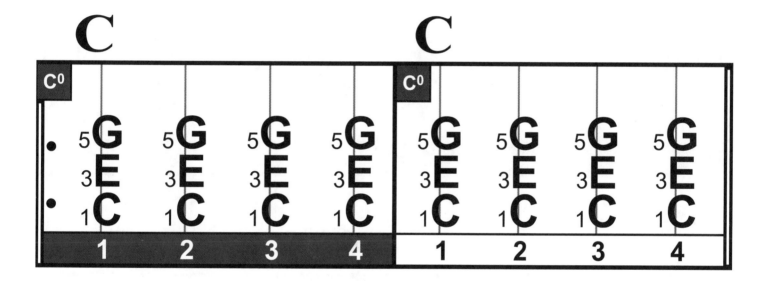

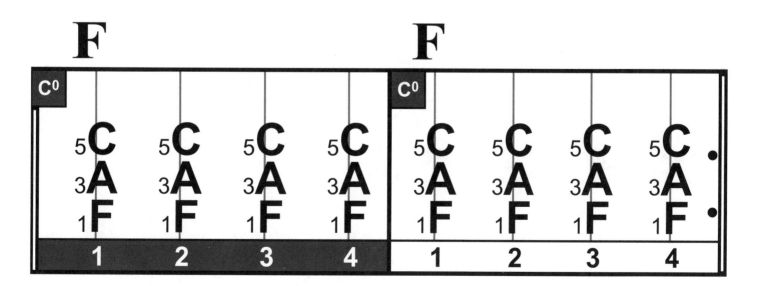

The 1- 5 Progression

In the same fashion as we did the 1 – 4 progression you will no learn a 1 – 5 progression. The G chord is five scale degrees above the root chord C. This progression is also in quester note timing. You can also play this in other timings such as half note, whole note and eighth note timings.

When communicating with other musicians it is important to understand how progressions are referenced. Think about the musical alphabet and use that as a guide for understanding the distance from chord to chord in progressions. An example is G is five scale degrees after C, that is why this is a 1 – 5 progression. The 1 – 5 progression in E would be E to B chords because B is five scale degrees higher then E in the musical alphabet.

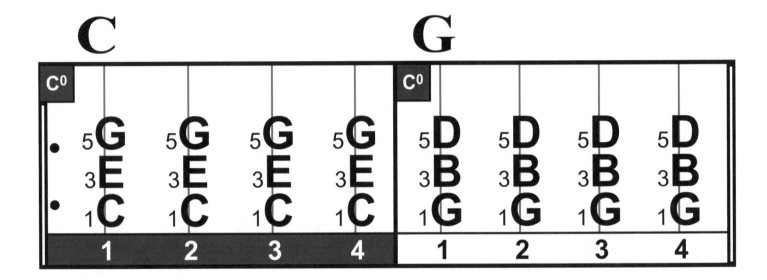

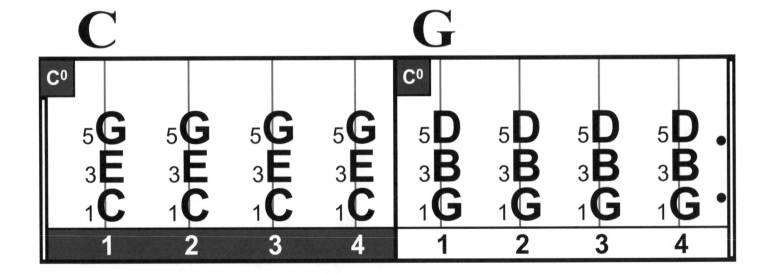

Adding Bass Notes

Now lets add the left hand bass notes to all the chords you played in the previous two chord progressions. The left hand notes add a bass element to the chords sound that makes the chord full and rich sounding. You can experiment moving the chord and bass notes to different octave ranges and hear how it changes the sound. In addition to playing the bass note and chord together you can play the bass notes and chords back and forth in a left hand right hand pattern. Also try holding the left hand down in whole notes while playing the right hand in quester notes as a variation.

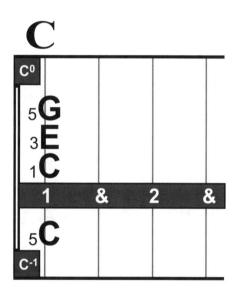

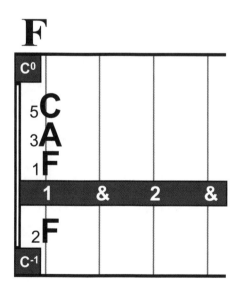

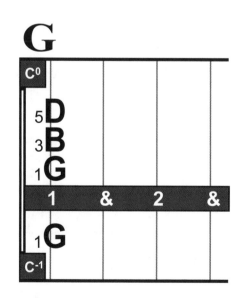

Chord Exercise
Arpeggio Chord Pattern

An arpeggio is the notes of a chord played in a row instead of playing them all together. This is a common way piano players play progressions in songs. By accenting different notes within each chord you can give a chord progression a distinct sound. Practice the pattern below and then we will use the pattern in some progressions and apply it in a song fashion.

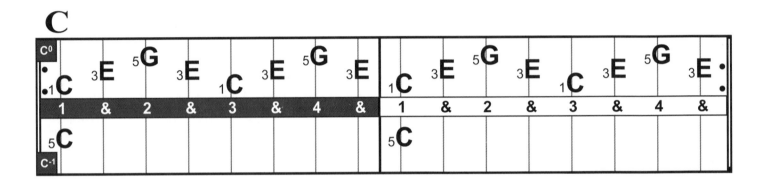

Arpeggio Chord Pattern 1 – 4 Progression

Play the arpeggio chord pattern with the 1 - 4 progression below. Take note that the left hand bass notes are whole notes that should be held for four beats each.

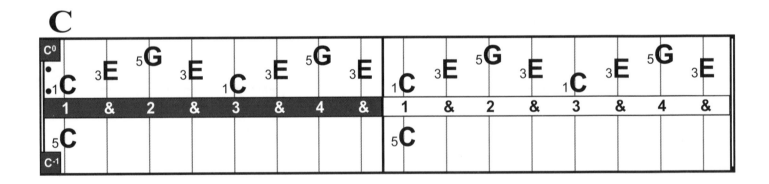

Arpeggio Chord Pattern 1 – 5 Progression

Now you will apply the arpeggio pattern to the 1 – 5 chord progression. Many songs are written using just these two chords so make sure to learn this progression and then experiment making your own variations of the arpeggio pattern.

C

1	&	2	&	3	&	4	&	1	&	2	&	3	&	4	&

G

1	&	2	&	3	&	4	&	1	&	2	&	3	&	4	&

C

1	&	2	&	3	&	4	&	1	&	2	&	3	&	4	&

G

1	&	2	&	3	&	4	&	1	&	2	&	3	&	4	&

Rocking Chord Technique

This is another popular chord playing technique. With the Rocking Chord Progression you will hold the bass root note while your right hand plays a rocking pattern. The right hand pattern is root then the 3rd and 5th together back and forth in a rocking fashion. Practice this pattern then we will apply it to the 1 – 4 and 1 – 5 chord progressions.

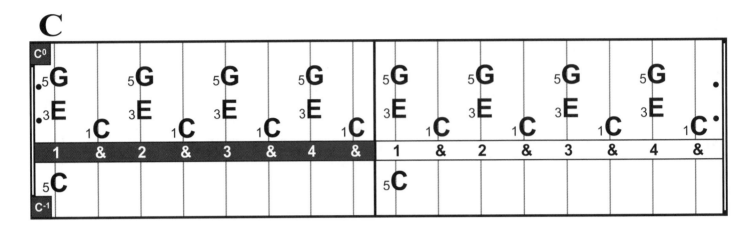

Rocking the Chords 1 – 4 Progression

In this lesson you will apply the rocking chord technique to the 1 – 4 progression. Start slow and build your speed up gradually.

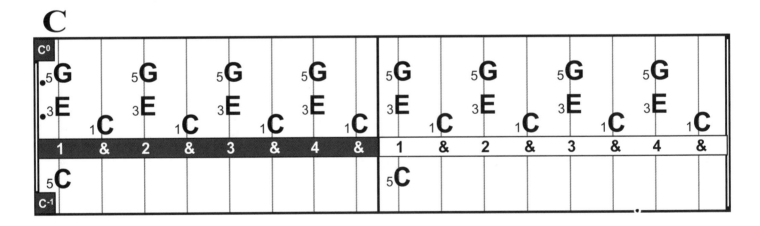

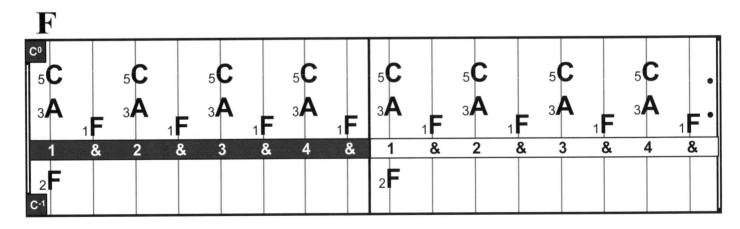

Applying the Rocking Chords
The 1- 5 Progression

Next apply the rocking chord technique to the 1 – 5 progression. Once you can play this pattern easily you should experiment and vary the pattern to create your own. Always try to be creative with your music.

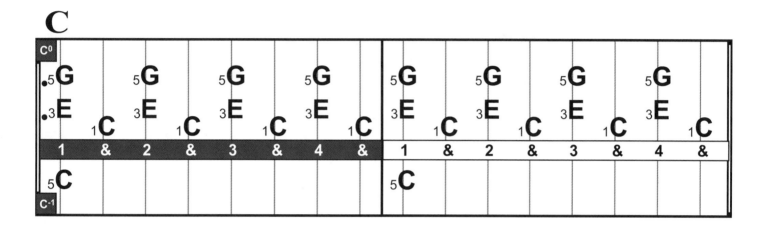

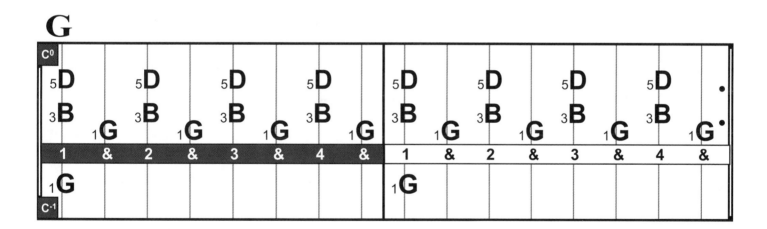

The 2 - 5 Progression
Introducing The D Major Chord

Here is another popular chord progression. In this chord progression notice that the left hand bass notes move to two different notes for each chord. This gives the chord progression movement. Also notice that the G chord uses a 2nd inversion which changes the order of the notes to D – G – B and the root note is in the middle. This makes the chord change from D to G a very easy transition.

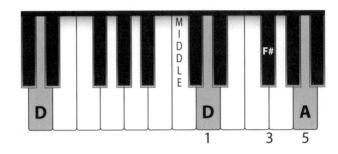

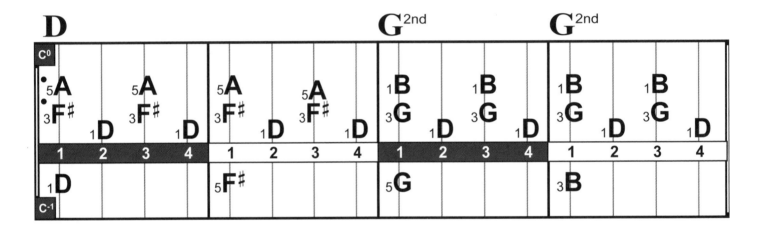

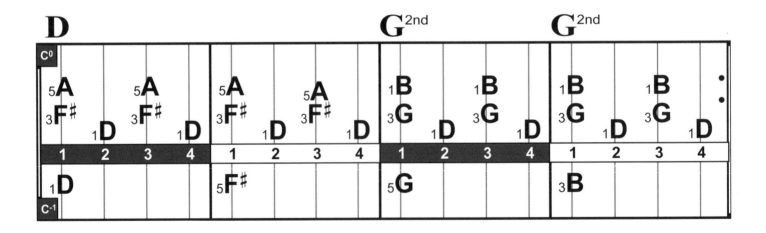

154

A Day at The Beach

This is a 1 – 4 – 5 progression from which thousands of songs use as the main structure. From the 50's to todays music there have been numerous hits written around this chord progression.

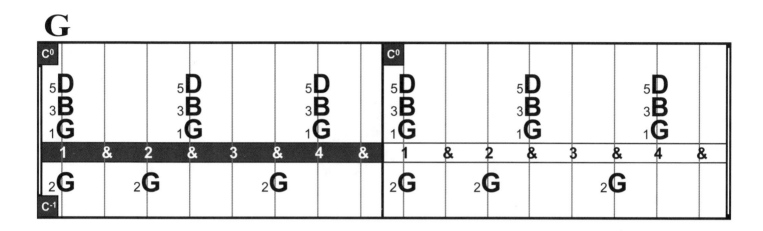

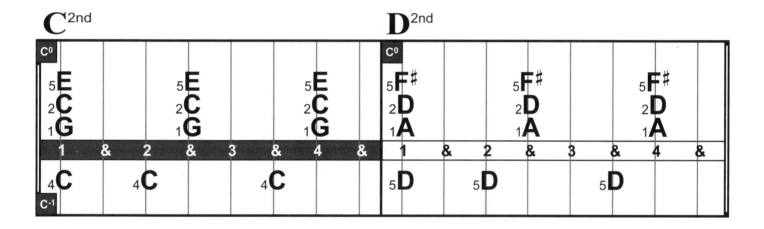

My Mojo Is Back
Shuffle Blues 1 - 4 - 5

The shuffle rhythm is an uneven blues timing that makes you sway with its moving feel. The left hand plays a moving rhythm while the right hand plays root 5th intervals. I recommend that you play the left hand by itself before putting both hands together because it is a bit challenging. The 1 – 4 – 5 progression is a standard for blues music so this is a must for your repertoire.

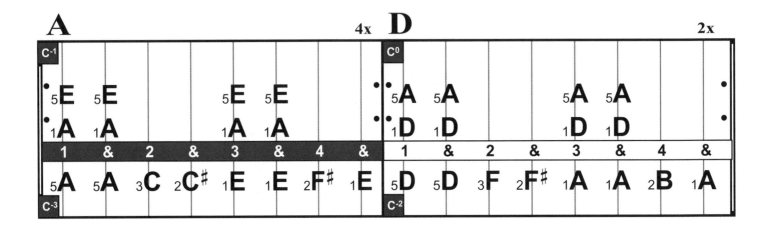

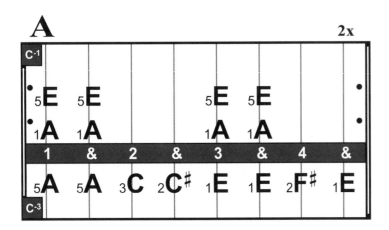

156

Royal Rock
1 - 5 - 6 - 4 Progression

The 1 – 5 – 6 – 4 progression is the most used progression for modern music over the past 20 years. Just about every one of the top rock and pop artists have one song that is using this structure and some have many. This is the 1 – 4 – 5 progression with an added 6th chord which is the relative minor chord. This is what makes this progression work so well.

C-I

	1	&	2	&	3	&	4	&
5G 3E 1C	•5G 3E •1C		5G 3E 1C		5G 3E 1C		5G 3E 1C		
5C				5C				

G-V

	1	&	2	&	3	&	4	&
5D 3B 1G	5D 3B 1G		5D 3B 1G		5D 3B 1G		5D 3B 1G		
1G				1G				

Am-VI

	1	&	2	&	3	&	4	&
5E 3C 1A	5E 3C 1A		5E 3C 1A		5E 3C 1A		5E 3C 1A		
1A				1A				

F-IV

	1	&	2	&	3	&	4	&
5C 3A 1F	5C 3A 1F		5C 3A 1F		5C 3A 1F		5C 3A 1F		
3F				3F				

Royal Rock
Inversion Version

Using inversions will help you make chord changes easy and seamlessly. It eliminates excessive hand movement. The inversions just take the notes of the chords and put them in different orders from top to bottom. Pay close attention to the fingerings for both hands to make the chord changes flow.

C-I

	1	&	2	&	3	&	4	&
C⁰	5G 3E 1C		5G 3E 1C	5G 3E 1C	5G 3E 1C		5G 3E 1C		
	5C				5C			
C-1								

G-V

	1	&	2	&	3	&	4	&
C⁰	5G 2D 1B		5G 2D 1B	5G 2D 1B	5G 2D 1B		5G 2D 1B		
	1G				1G			
C⁰								

Am-VI

	1	&	2	&	3	&	4	&
C⁰	5A 2E 1C		5A 2E 1C	5A 2E 1C	5A 2E 1C		5A 2E 1C		
	1A				1A			
C-1								

F-IV

	1	&	2	&	3	&	4	&
C⁰	5A 3F 1C		5A 3F 1C	5A 3F 1C	5A 3F 1C		5A 3F 1C		
	3F				3F			
C⁰								

Single Note Two Hand Riff

This is a fun riff that has both hands doing the same sequence of notes. You can try doing different octaves for each hand as well.

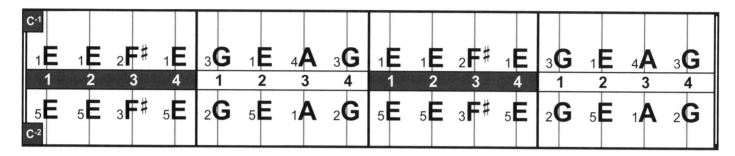

Blue Velvet

1 – 6 – 3 – 5 progression

Here is another popular chord progression. Pay close attention to the inversions for each chord. The left and right hands go back and forth creating a great rhythm.

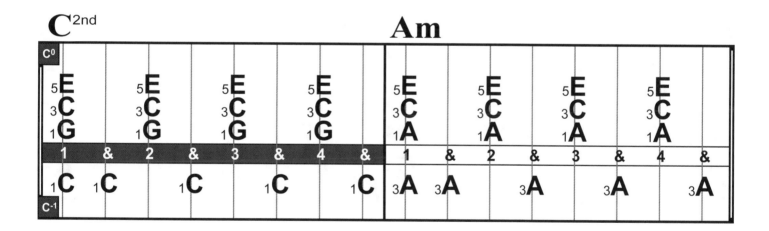

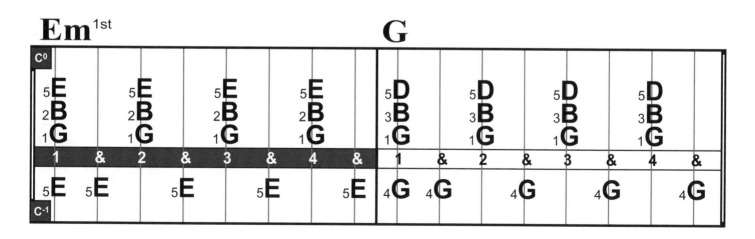

Black Pearl
Minor Chord Progression

The relative minor to C major is A minor. This chord progression is in the key of A minor and that means that you will use the same chords from C major since they are relative keys. You will learn more about relative minor theory in the course.

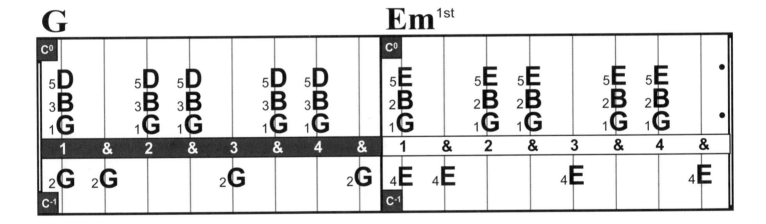

Blues In "A"
Left Hand Blues

Many times in blues the left hand will play a series of intervals to create a solid rhythm to play leads and melodies over. Here is a classic blues left hand pattern.

A-I

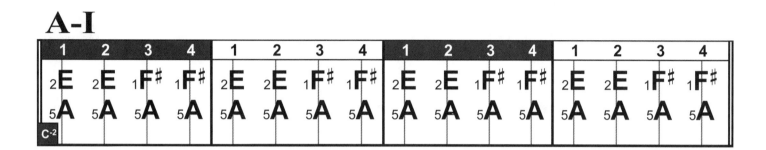

D-IV

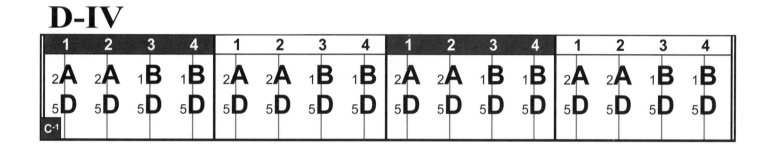

A-I

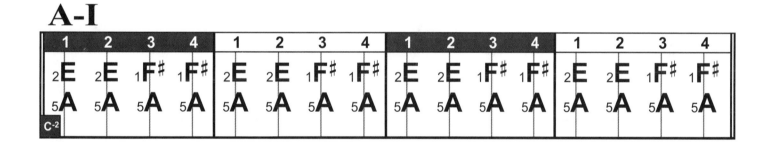

E-V   D-IV

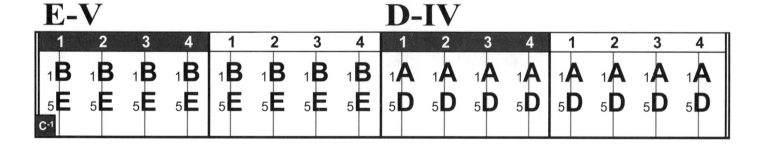

A-I

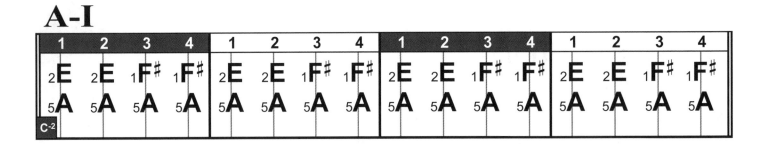

Street of Dreams

Here is another chord progression using quarter note timing. Pay close attention to the chord inversions and fingerings.

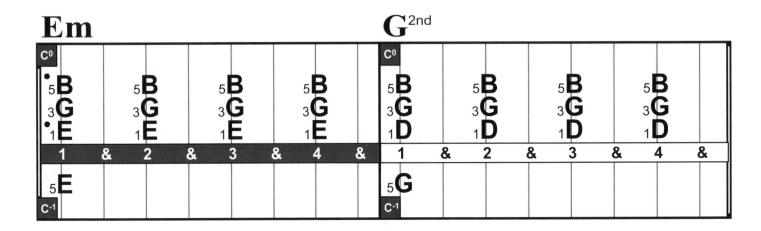

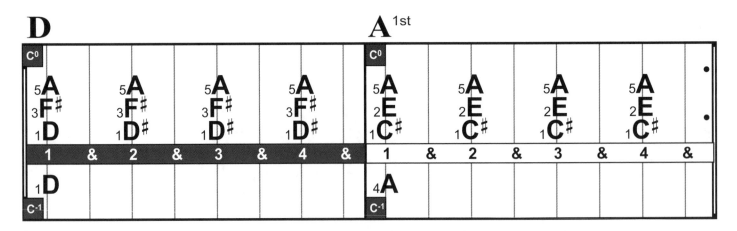

The A Blues Scale

Time to learn one of the most popular scales for improvising in rock and blues music. The blues scale has a flat 5 note that creates a great blues sound. This note is called the "Blues Tri-tone" It is a passing tone and you should not pause on the note.

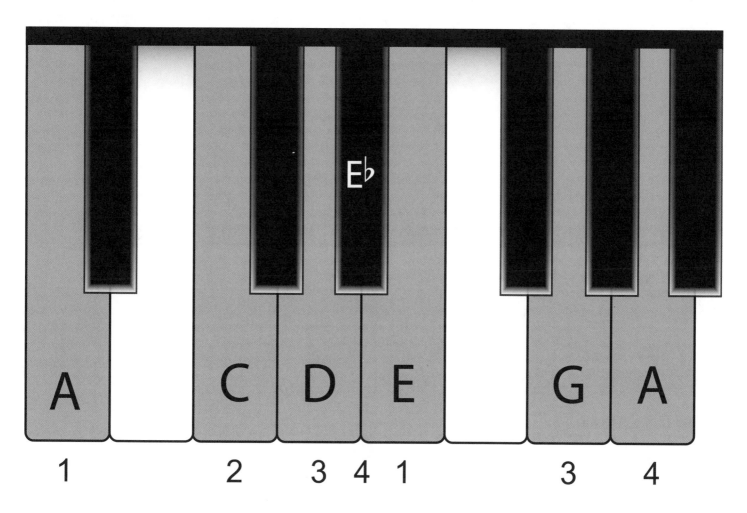

Cross Under

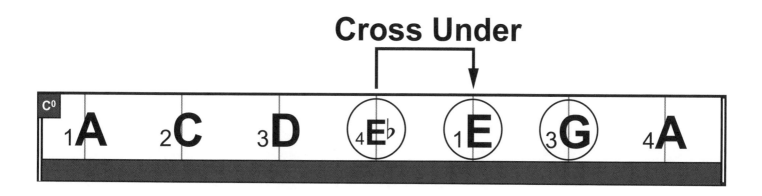

Playing The Blues
Blues Riffs

As you progress as a musician you will learn to improvise and make your own melodies and riffs. I wrote a few simple riffs using the A Blues scale to get you started. Once you have these under your fingers try to create your own riffs using the Blues scale. Always write down your creations so you don't forget you ideas..

First Section

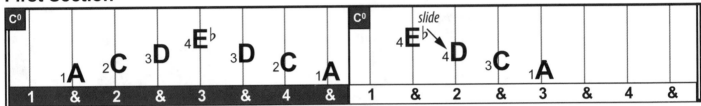

Second Section

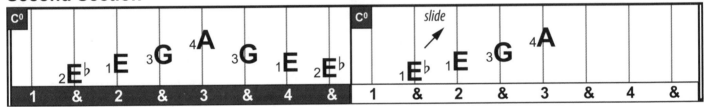

Slide Up & Down

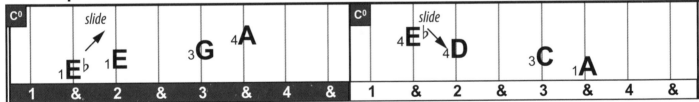

The 1 - 6 - 4 - 5 Progression
The 4 Chord Song Part 2

You previously learned the 1 – 5 - 6 - 4 progression and I told you that this was the most popular progression of modern times. The sister to this progression that is still used today but was a bit more popular back in the 50's and 60's is the 1 – 6 – 4 – 5 progression. The same chords are used just in a different order giving the progression its own unique sound.

C-I

C⁰								
•₅G		₅G	₅G		₅G	₅G		
₃E		₃E	₃E		₃E	₃E		
•₁C		₁C	₁C		₁C	₁C		
1	**&**	**2**	**&**	**3**	**&**	**4**	**&**	
₁C	₁C			₁C			₅C	
C⁻²								

Am-VI

₅E		₅E	₅E		₅E	₅E	
₃C		₃C	₃C		₃C	₃C	
₁A		₁A	₁A		₁A	₁A	
1	**&**	**2**	**&**	**3**	**&**	**4**	**&**
₃A	₃A			₃A			₃A

F-IV

C⁰								
₅C		₅C	₅C		₅C	₅C		
₃A		₃A	₃A		₃A	₃A		
₁F		₁F	₁F		₁F	₁F		
1	**&**	**2**	**&**	**3**	**&**	**4**	**&**	
₅F	₅F			₅F			₅F	
C⁻²								

G-V

₅D		₅D	₅D		₅D	₅D	
₃B		₃B	₃B		₃B	₃B	
₁G		₁G	₁G		₁G	₁G	
1	**&**	**2**	**&**	**3**	**&**	**4**	**&**
₄G	₄G			₄G			₄G

Rock Climbing Song Progression

This progression has a bass note sequence that gets higher in pitch each note in song order, which gives the song a climbing feel. Pay close attention to the chord inversions and fingerings. Make sure to play this with the audio backing tracks to create a full band sound. You can also experiment with variations in the pattern and create your own sound.

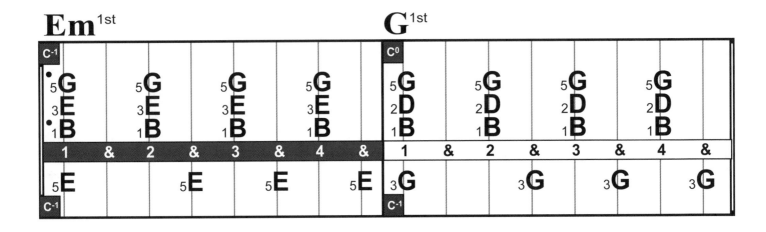

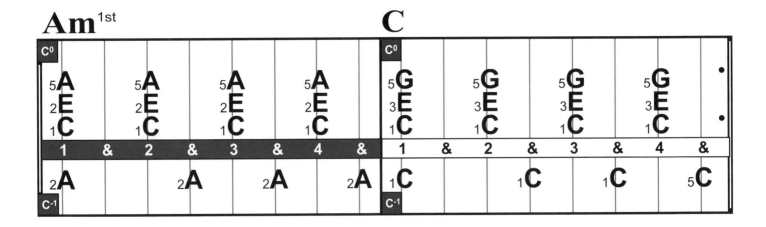

House of The Rising Sun

This is a classic 60s rock song written and performed by the animals back in 1964 and has stood the test of time because many bands still cover this song. The rhythm is slightly different then you have learned so far. It is counted 123, 123, 123, 123 as you play each chord. Hold the root bass note for each three beat measure.

Am

5E	5E	5E	5E	5E	5E
3C	3C	3C	3C	3C	3C
1A	1A	1A	1A	1A	1A

1 & 2 & 3 &

1A
5A

C

5E	5E	5E	5E	5E	5E
3C	3C	3C	3C	3C	3C
1G	1G	1G	1G	1G	1G

1 & 2 & 3 &

4C

D

5D	5D	5D	5D	5D	5D
3A	3A	3A	3A	3A	3A
1F#	1F#	1F#	1F#	1F#	1F#

1 & 2 & 3 &

3D

F

5C	5C	5C	5C	5C	5C
3A	3A	3A	3A	3A	3A
1F	1F	1F	1F	1F	1F

1 & 2 & 3 &

2F

Am

5E	5E	5E	5E	5E	5E
3C	3C	3C	3C	3C	3C
1A	1A	1A	1A	1A	1A

1 & 2 & 3 &

1A
5A

C

5E	5E	5E	5E	5E	5E
3C	3C	3C	3C	3C	3C
1G	1G	1G	1G	1G	1G

1 & 2 & 3 &

4C

E

• 5E	5E	5E	5E	5E	5E •
3B	3B	3B	3B	3B	3B
• 1G#	1G#	1G#	1G#	1G#	1G# •

1 & 2 & 3 &

3E

2x **Am**

5E	5E	5E	5E	5E	5E
3C	3C	3C	3C	3C	3C
1A	1A	1A	1A	1A	1A

1 & 2 & 3 &

1A
5A

167

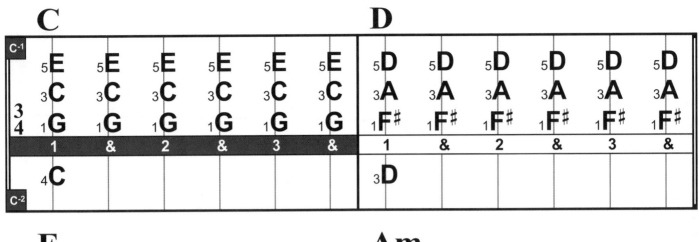

Julian's Theme

This is a more complex song progression. Notice there is a dominant 7th chord in the progression, this chord is found most in songs on the 5th degree of the chord scale. In this case the song is in the key of F and the 5th degree is C so that is why there is a C7th chord in the progression. The rhythm follows a right / left rocking pattern.

Julian's Theme

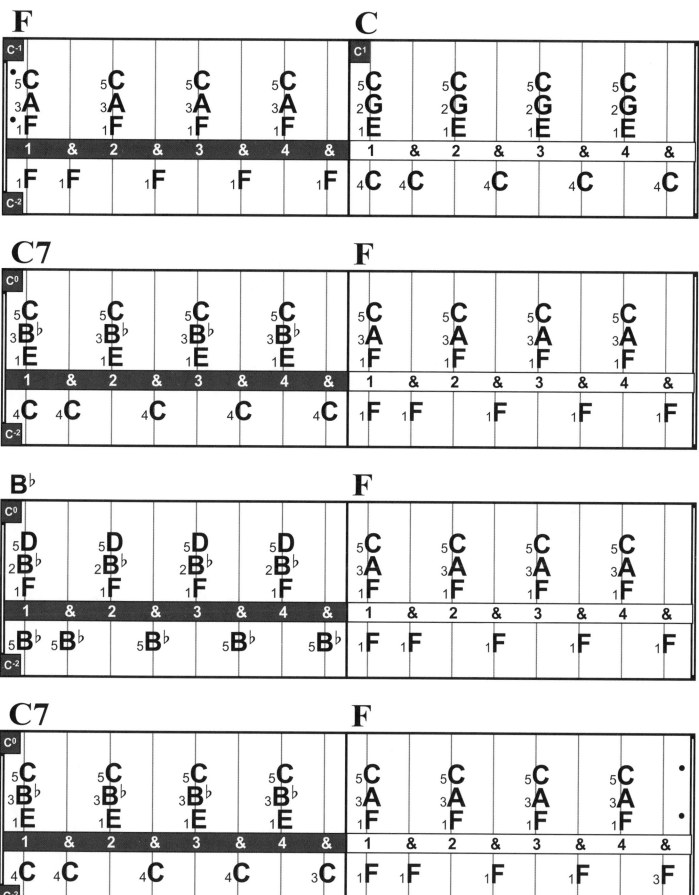

Chord Glossary

C

  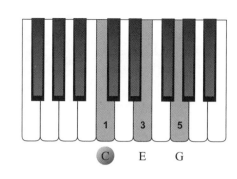

C E G

C+

  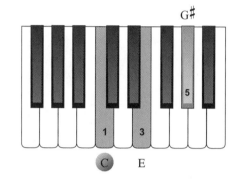

G#
C E

Csus⁴

   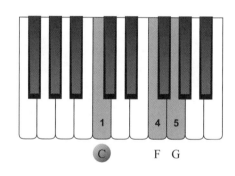

C F G

C6

  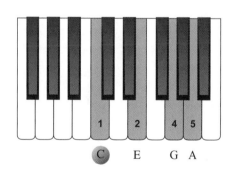

C E G A

C7

  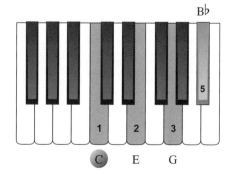

B♭
C E G

D

 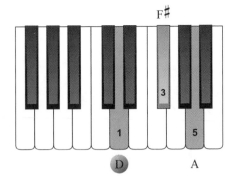

D+

 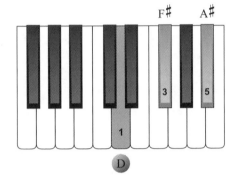

Dsus⁴

 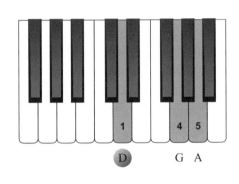

D6

 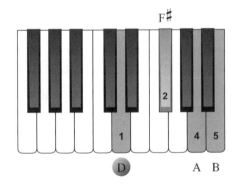

D7

 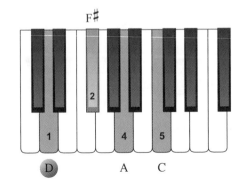

E♭

  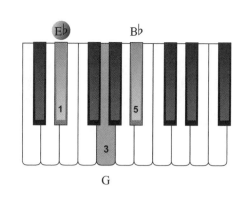

E♭+

 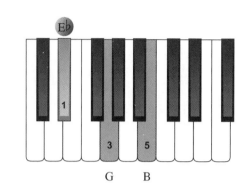

E♭sus⁴

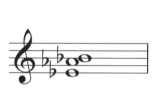  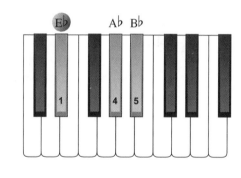

E♭6

  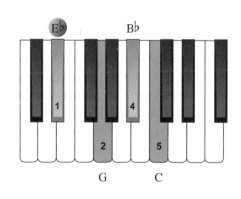

E♭7

  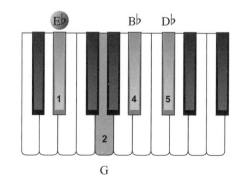

173

E

  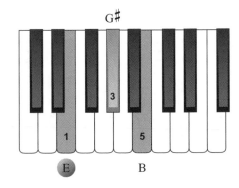

E+

  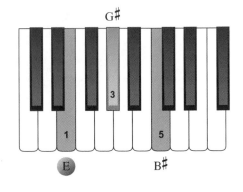

Esus⁴

  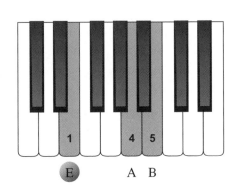

E6

  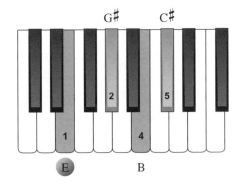

E7

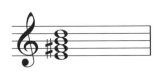  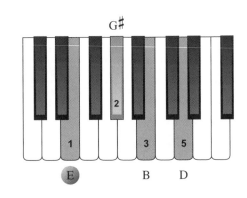

174

F

  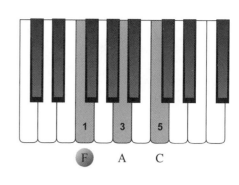

F+

  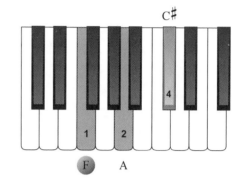

Fsus⁴

  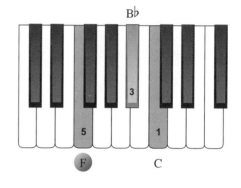

F6

  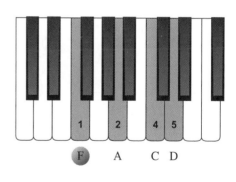

F7

  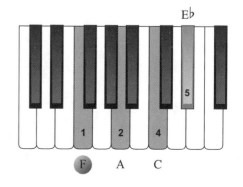

175

G

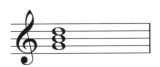  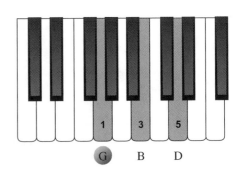

G+

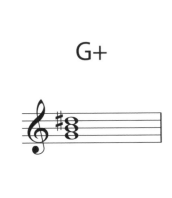  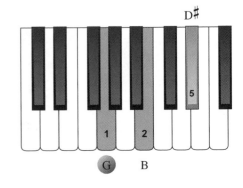

Gsus^4

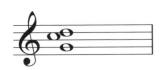  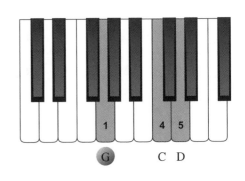

G6

  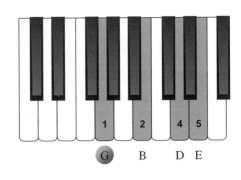

G7

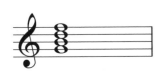  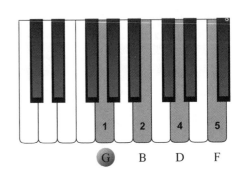

A♭

  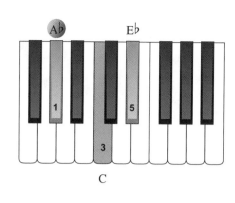

A♭+

  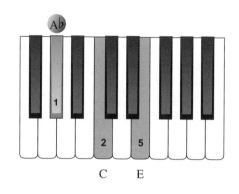

A♭sus⁴

  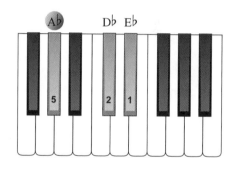

A♭6

  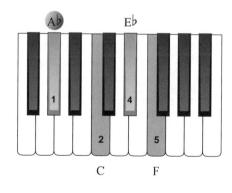

A♭7

  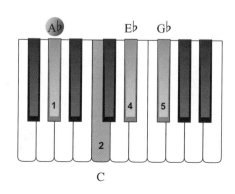

A

A+

Asus⁴

A6

A7

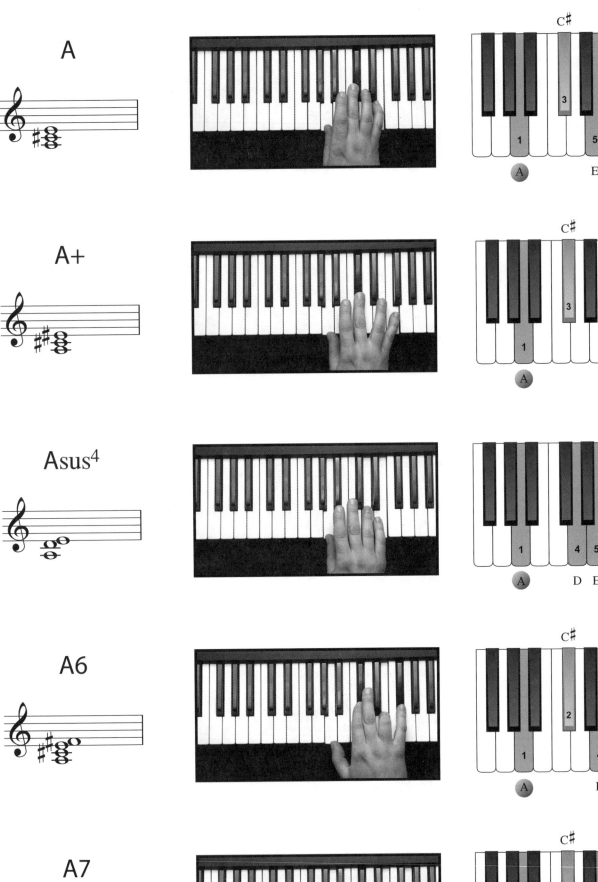

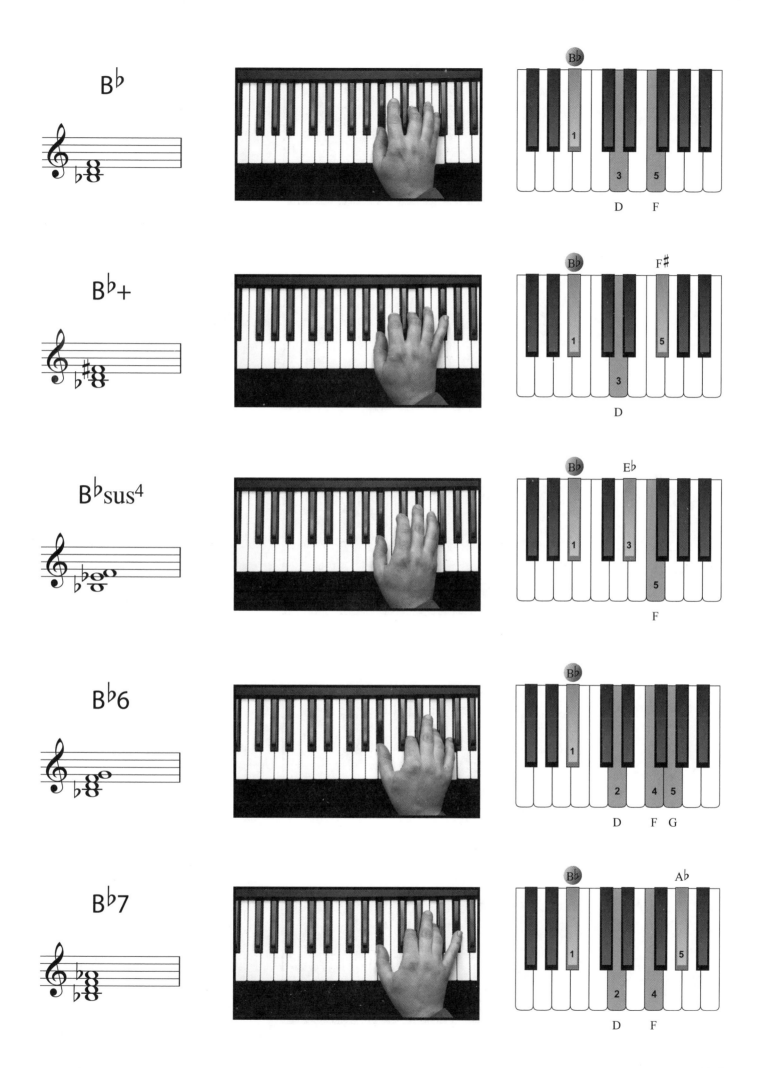

B♭

B♭+

B♭sus⁴

B♭6

B♭7

179

B

B+

Bsus⁴

B6

B7

Relative Minor Scales

Relative keys are major and minor scales that share the same key signature. Relative scales consist of the same exact notes. The difference is which note begins the scale; a minor scale begins on the sixth note of its relative major: for example, C major and A minor are relative keys - both have no accidentals. See the diagram below:

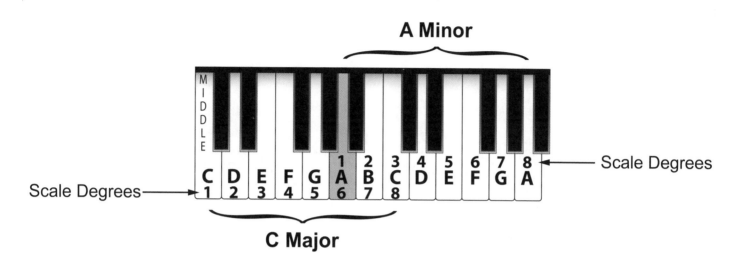

Here are all of the major and relative minor scales for you to play through:

D Major

B Minor

A Major

F♯ Minor

E Major

C♯ Minor

B Major

G♯ Minor

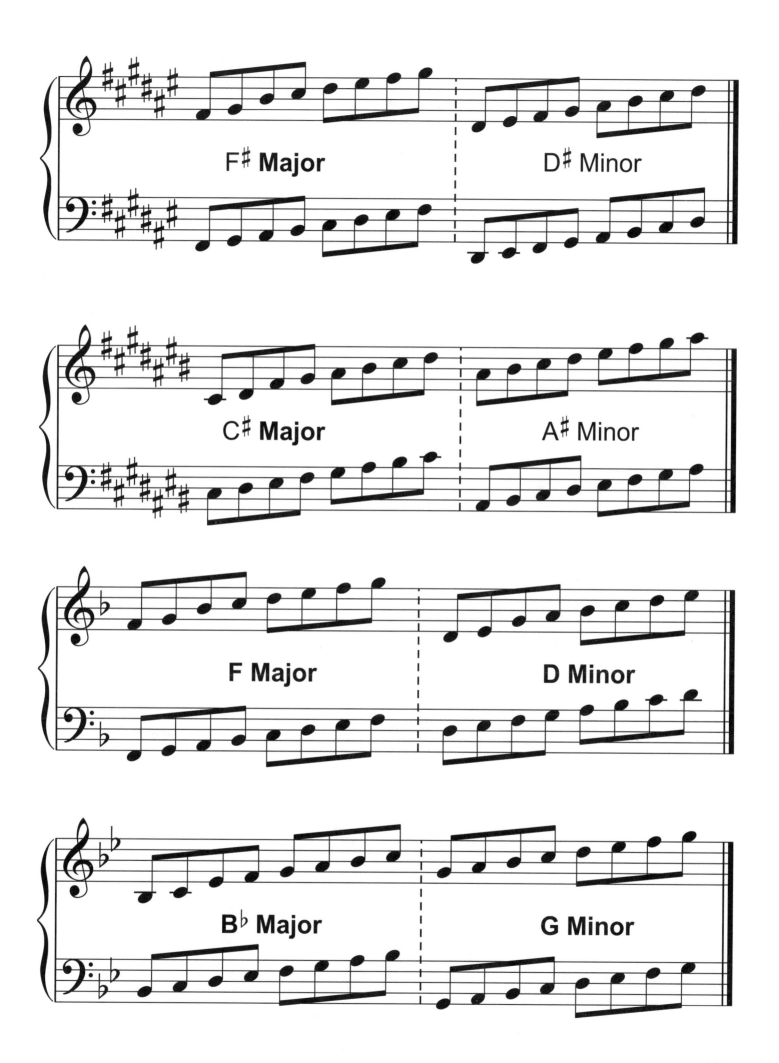

F# Major

D# Minor

C# Major

A# Minor

F Major

D Minor

B♭ Major

G Minor

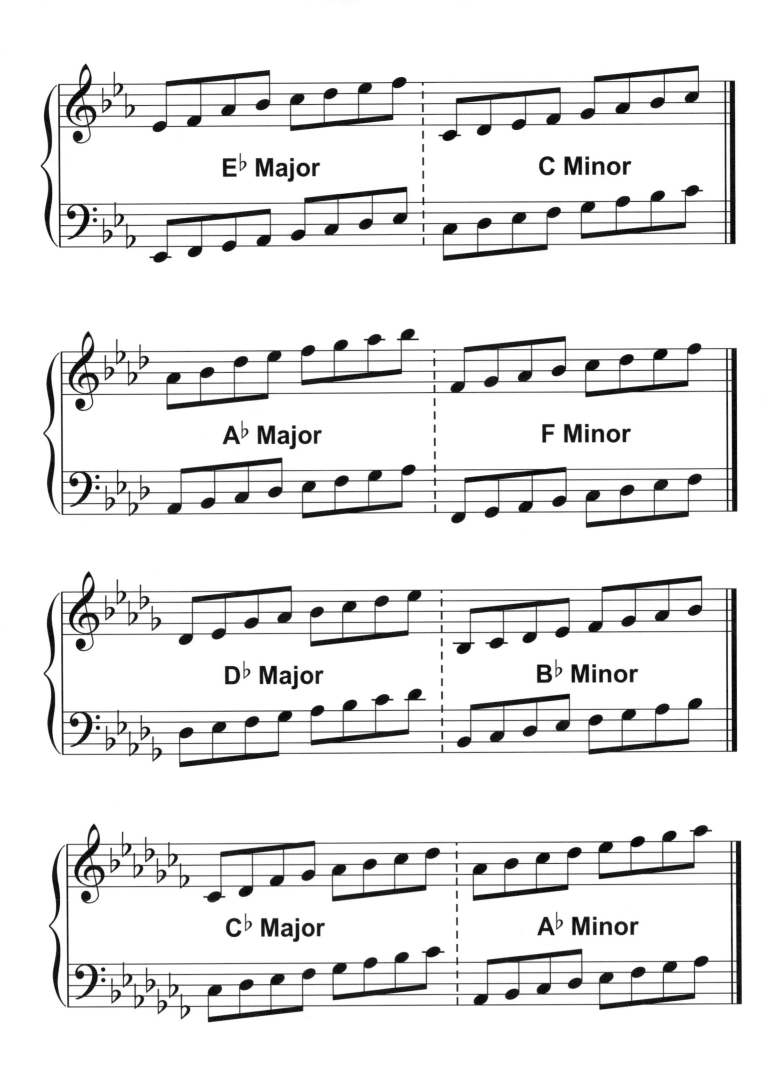

About the Author

John McCarthy
Creator of
The Rock House Method

John is the creator of The Rock House Method®, the world's leading musical instruction system. Over his 25 plus year career, he has written, produced and/or appeared in more than 100 instructional products. Millions of people around the world have learned to play music using John's easy-to-follow, accelerated programs.

John is a virtuoso musician who has worked with some of the industry's most legendary musicians. He has the ability to break down, teach and communicate music in a manner that motivates and inspires others to achieve their dreams of playing an instrument.

As a musician and songwriter, John blends together a unique style of rock, metal, funk and blues in a collage of melodic compositions. Throughout his career, John has recorded and performed with renowned musicians including Doug Wimbish (Joe Satriani, Living Colour, The Rolling Stones, Madonna, Annie Lennox), Grammy Winner Leo Nocentelli, Rock & Roll Hall of Fame inductees Bernie Worrell and Jerome "Big Foot" Brailey, Freekbass, Gary Hoey, Bobby Kimball, David Ellefson (founding member of seven time Grammy nominee Megadeth), Will Calhoun (B.B. King, Mick Jagger and Paul Simon), Gus G of Ozzy and many more.

To get more information about John McCarthy, his music and instructional products visit RockHouseSchool.com.

MEMBER NUMBER

To download the lesson video and audio backingtracks that correspond with this book us the member number and register at RockHouseMethod.com

MEMBER
ME442346